Robert Carrier's
Gourmet Vegetarian

B☘XTREE

GRANADA TELEVISION

First published in Great Britain in 1994
by Boxtree Limited

3 4 5 6 7 8 9 10

A CIP catalogue entry for this book is available from
the British Library

ISBN 1 85283 952 X

Designed by Geoff Hayes
Photography by Michelle Garratt, except p. 68
(Roy Rich); pp. 69, 72-3 & 160 (John Stewart); and
p. 100 (Andy Seymour); reproduced by courtesy of
Robert Carrier.

Printed and bound in the UK by
Bath Press Colourbooks for

Boxtree Limited
Broadwall House
21 Broadwall
London SE1 9PL

Contents

Guide to Healthy Eating

It wasn't so long ago that vegetarians were looked upon in many restaurants as cranky 'non-foodies' who were often foisted off with a cheese omelette and a helping or two of whatever vegetables were in the steam tray. Today, all that has changed, and for the better. Vegetable and rice and pasta dishes are top choices on the menus of today's trendier restaurants and more and more people – the young, particularly – are veering towards a healthy vegetarian way of eating. And many, like myself, are choosing the semi-vegetarian way: choosing complete vegetarian meals two or three days per week, varying their diets occasionally with fish, shellfish or farm-raised poultry.

I find that at home I tend to rely more and more on wonderful Mediterranean dishes of grilled summer vegetables garnished with a few chick peas and mung beans for added protein, sprigs of fresh herbs for extra vitamins and chopped garlic and extra virgin olive oil for added flavour.

At dinner parties I like to serve pasta dishes good enough to die for: penne al vodka (fat tubes of pasta with a creamy vodka-and-lemon-infused tomato sauce; pasta con verdure (flat egg noodles cooked in vegetable stock and served with crisp cooked green vegetables) and thin shavings of grana (fresh Parmesan cheese) … and glamorous stir-fries of glittering vegetables infused with soy, mirin (Japanese rice wine) and finely chopped ginger, garlic and lemon grass for a unique Far Eastern flavour.

It is estimated that there are currently about 3 million people in this country who don't eat meat, and the number is growing day by day. Many people give up meat or fish on moral or compassionate grounds, but probably the main reason why people go on a vegetarian diet – or semi-vegetarian, eating only the occasional white meat, fish or shellfish – is because they are caught up in the new search for a healthy, more active and longer life. Modern science has taught us that we really *are* what we eat. Or, at least, that what we eat affects our health as well as our mental energy and our well-being.

A vegetarian plant-based diet – featuring exciting meals such as grilled Italian bread topped with a white bean purée and rocket, lentils tossed with colourful cubes of roasted vegetables, basmati rice studded with raisins and pine-nuts and tamales bursting with pumpkin and grilled peppers – is naturally low in saturated fats (found mainly in meat and dairy products). It is a diet high in healthy complex carbohydrate foods – the very carbohydrates that doctors say should form the basis of our daily diet – whole-wheat bread, rice and other grains, pasta, dried beans, peas and lentils, and especially fresh vegetables and fruits. These complex carbohydrate-rich plant-based foods provide the needed bulk for our daily diet; they are rich in fibre and in the right combination are also high in needed protein.

Helping People Make Healthier Choices

Recent scientific studies show us that a diet rich in fresh vegetables and fruits, grains and nuts provides us with more energy, fewer calories and lower blood cholesterol levels; with less risk of digestive disorders, heart disease and certain forms of cancer; and a lesser risk of obesity and diabetes.

Now, none of us want to suffer from heart disease, cancer or diabetes. We all want to be relatively slim and energetic. We all love the colour and freshness of just-grilled vegetables; pastas in all their variety; quick stir-fries of crisp and tasty goodness. So it is obvious that for health reasons – and for economy reasons – it is time for us all to become vegetarians at least two or three times a week. The benefit to our health will be enormous. For what we eat affects the quality of our life.

Making the Food Choices That Encourage Good Health

The purpose of good and healthy eating is to increase our longevity and our bodily strength ... and some think that it also purifies our minds and our very state of being. I won't go as far as claiming that eating a plate of rice and beans every day will change my way of thinking or alter my state of being, but I do find that bingeing-out on difficult-to-digest foods tends to make my mind dull and my body tired and heavy. And what is more important, I find that I don't have the energy that I need to think things out and to make important decisions. It is then that I go 'gourmet vegetarian' in a big way and build my meals around a high carbohydrate food such as rice, cracked wheat or couscous. Sometimes the main course will be pasta-based, or a dish of green lentils, chick peas and beans; a quick stir-fry of crisp tasty vegetables or an open vegetable tart or pizza. With such a centrepiece as the focal point of the meal, I just add a salad of raw and cooked vegetables (the inclusion of one or two lightly cooked vegetables – courgettes, marrow, butternut pumpkin, potatoes, leeks, carrots, turnips or swedes – in a salad of leafy greens makes it more satisfying and attractive). You can finish off the meal with fresh fruit and a sorbet, or, for a richer menu, with one of the quick and easy recipes in the desserts chapter. Make sure you vary your diet by experimenting with new foods, new recipes, new fruits and vegetables. This will give you a varied and healthy diet.

Some Simple Starters

Precede your meal, if you like, with baked eggs in individual ramekins, or more imaginatively, in vegetable containers made of hollowed-out ripe tomatoes or halved green and yellow peppers.

Let soups star as a light starter: hot black bean soup with diced croûtons for texture; a frothy blend of pumpkin and leek, softened with cream; or a bowl of chilled vegetable soup with cut-outs of paper-thin vegetables as an attractive and healthy garnish.

Make pitta-based pizzas your quick and easy first course; try individual cheese soufflés with different vegetable garnishes as an intriguing and glamorous starter; or fall back on individual versions of Mediterranean salads or a colourful trio of grilled fresh vegetables served cold with a vinaigrette – especially attractive if garnished with a few chick peas, some alfalfa sprouts and snippets of fresh coriander, fennel, basil or tarragon.

I like, too, to begin a vegetarian meal with a hot slice – or an individual pastry shell – of vegetable quiche or flan: an Italian spinach tart (based on the recipe for Italian gnocchi), a Roquefort cream quiche or a French onion tart. Go colour – and texture – mad with a pepper pissaladière, using bright yellow, red and green pepper strips for a garnish on the traditional Provençal tomato and onion tart. Or go way out with a jewel-like spring vegetable tart (a painter's palette of lightly poached spring onions, mini patty-pan squash, sliced courgettes and carrots), glazed with a saffron-flavoured butter sauce.

Or give them the best little cucumber salad in the world. The secret is easy: just marinate the thinly sliced cucumbers in two different salad dressings (one to take away the bitter juices of the cucumber, the second to lend an intense, brilliantly herby flavour). Serve crudités with three spanking fresh dips: (1) garlic- and herb-flavoured Greek yogurt or fromage frais; (2) Mexican guacamole; and (3) tomato salsa.

Quick and Informal Snacks, Lunches and Suppers

For quick and informal suppers and lunches, go the bread route with slices of grilled focaccia, ciabatta, whole-grain bread or rye, topped with a variety of vegetarian toppings: (1) grilled aubergine slices and raw tomatoes topped with pesto sauces and slivers of fresh basil; (2) sautéed sliced mixed peppers (red, yellow and green), topped with Mexican corn salsa; (3) cubes of peeled and seeded ripe tomatoes marinated in extra-virgin olive oil sparked with crushed dried chillies and snippets of fresh basil; or (4) *pan bagna* – large baps, cut in half, with cut sides toasted until crisp, filled with a salade niçoise (complete with sliced hard-boiled eggs and black olives) in an olive dressing.

Make savoury croustades by hollowing out bread rolls, brushing them with melted butter or oil, seasoning them with freshly grated Parmesan cheese and paprika and baking them in a hot oven until crisp and golden. Then fill them with: (1) diced stir-fried tofu and crisp vegetables; (2) diced 'beefsteak' tomato and cooked asparagus with green peas and sliced spring onions in a vinaigrette sauce, 'greened' with chopped fresh herbs and garlic; or (3) soft scrambled eggs garnished with sautéed sliced mushrooms and thin strips of red pimento. Or make little baked filo pastry cups and fill them with: (1) a Greek salad of diced tomatoes, green peppers, green beans and feta cheese, garnished with black olives; (2) a saffron rice salad garnished with diced raw mushroom, avocado, cucumber and tomato tossed in a garlicky dressing; or (3) Chinese fried rice with diced onion, wild mushroom, tofu and beansprouts, flavoured with soy and mirin.

Here are the Healthy Foods

Green leaves of all kinds (kale, Swiss chard, spinach, watercress, parsley), tossed in butter or extra-virgin olive oil. Rich in folic acid, vitamin C, vitamin E.

Grains of all kinds (barley, white rice, brown rice, couscous, kasha, bulghur, corn (polenta), steamed or boiled and then tossed with seasonings and a little oil or butter. Delicious with added poached or grilled vegetables. Rich in vitamin B1, folic acid, vitamin E, iron, potassium, fibre.

Green vegetables (asparagus, broccoli, peas, spring greens, Brussels sprouts, green beans, butter beans and spinach), blanched and then tossed in butter or oil with a little crumbled vegetable stock cube for added flavour. Rich in vitamins B2, B3, B6, vitamin C, vitamin E, calcium.

Dried pulse vegetables (haricot beans, adzuki beans, lentils, chick peas, black beans, dried peas and black-eyed beans), pre-soaked and then simmered in a little oil and water with finely chopped garlic, onion, flat-leafed parsley and fresh coriander and your choice of seasonings: (1) saffron, cinnamon, paprika and cayenne; (2) finely chopped fresh ginger, garlic and lemon grass; or (3) cooked as above and then tossed, when cool, with a well-flavoured vinaigrette dressing. Rich in vitamins B1, B2, B3, B6, folic acid, iron, calcium, zinc, potassium, fibre.

Soya beans, soy sauce, tofu. Rich in vitamins B1, B3, B6, vitamin E, iron, calcium.
Sweet potatoes. Rich in vitamin B6, folic acid, vitamin C, vitamin E.

Green leaves of all descriptions (Little Gem lettuce, Cos lettuce, frisée, batavia, radicchió, young spinach leaves, endive, rocket, arugula, and sprigs of fresh basil, fennel, coriander, french tarragon and flat-leafed parsley) make wonderful mixed salads when tossed in a well-flavoured vinaigrette dressing.

Cheeses. Rich in vitamins B2, B3, B6, folic acid, calcium, zinc.

Whole-wheat flour, breads and pasta. Rich in vitamins B1, B3, vitamin E, iron, zinc, fibre.

Nuts Rich in vitamins B1, B2, B6, folic acid, vitamin E, calcium, zinc.

Wheat-germ oil, olive oil, corn oil, peanut oil, palm oil, soya oil, sunflower oil, safflower oil. Rich in vitamin E.

Fresh fruit salads and sorbets (apricots, guavas, mangoes, blackcurrants, straw-berries, raspberries, blueberries, gooseberries, nectarines, peaches, pears, apples, lychees, melon, pineapple and all citrus fruits). Wonderful alone or in colourful combinations. Rich in vitamin C.

Yogurt Yogurt is most popular with the people of Russia and the Balkan countries, known for their long lives. Elie Metchnikoff, a Russian gerontologist, first indicated the link between a yogurt-rich diet and long life (increased longevity). In the nineteenth century he created the theory of auto-intoxication, which stated that it is possible for the contents of the colon to enter the bloodstream and thereby poison the entire body. Yogurt produces lactic acid, which destroys the bacteria responsible for the putrefaction of food in the large intestine, one of the main causes of fatigue, disease and premature ageing. It has natural antibiotic properties strong enough to kill certain amoebas and virulent bacteria, such as staphylococcus, streptococcus, and even typhus.
Yogurt is rich in proteins, minerals, enzymes and most known vitamins, including B12.

Going Vegetarian Gradually

If you are thinking of going vegetarian, do it gradually by cutting down portion sizes of meat, poultry, fish and shellfish products on your plate and increasing portion sizes of vegetables, pulses, pasta, rice and other grains.

Gradually, make all breakfasts and lunches plant-based meals. Then remove flesh-based dinner main courses every other day and substitute high-protein plant foods such as pulse vegetables combined with rice. Make one main course per week a pasta dish, with a vegetable sauce or added vegetables; at another meal make it a casserole of vegetables. In this way, you will be eating vegetarian before you know it.

Simple Ways with Vegetable Protein
Once or twice a week make a cottage pie with easy to use TVP, a pasta 'bolognese' using a Quorn, or a vegetarian stir-fry of vegetable and cubes of fresh tofu. Or, frankly, forget the meat substitutes and make a French onion tart, a pepper pissaladière or a Roquefort cream quiche (see recipes on pages 211, 208 and 209.) Nothing could be easier. Or more delicious.

Fresh Vegetable Primer

Artichoke, Globe
In Rome, tender young artichokes are often cooked with olive oil, lemon and herbs, *à la Romana*, and served as a marvellously flavoured hot or cold hors d'œuvre. I like artichoke hearts done in this manner, too, flavoured with a little finely chopped garlic and oregano. In France, artichokes au vin blanc top the bill, the artichokes simmered in dry white wine with a little olive oil and seasonings. Artichokes *à la Provençale*, *à la Barigoule*, or *à la Grècque* are all exalted variations on this basic theme.

There are so many ways to serve this delicate, nutty-flavoured vegetable – rich in iron, mineral salts and iodine – that I cannot understand why so many people consider it an acquired taste. I like artichokes baked, fried, stuffed, puréed with rich cream and even in a soup. But my favourite way of dealing with them is to cook them in boiling water with a little salt, olive oil and lemon juice and serve them either cold with a vinaigrette sauce, or hot with a hollandaise sauce (or melted butter flavoured with salt and lemon juice), as a first course.

Artichoke
To prepare globe artichokes
1 With a strong, sharp knife, slice all the leaves off the artichoke level with the tips of the shortest ones. Strip away any tough outer leaves. Trim the base and stem.
2 With a sharp-edged teaspoon, scoop and scrape out the fuzzy chokes, taking care not to leave a single fibre. Remember that an artichoke is the flower bud of a thistle and that these fibres are not called 'chokes' for nothing.
3 While you are working on the artichoke, keep dipping it into a bowl of water heavily acidulated with lemon juice. Do this each time you open a fresh surface to prevent it

turning brown. The artichoke contains peroxides and oxidizing enzymes which cause it (and any steel utensil used with it) to discolour very quickly when exposed to the air. This is not dangerous, but it makes the artichoke look unattractive and spoils its flavour.

To boil globe artichokes
1 To a large saucepan of water, add a handful of salt and some lemon juice (or a squeezed-out lemon half) and bring to the boil.
2 Immerse the artichokes and simmer for 30–40 minutes or until you can pull a leaf out easily.
3 Lift out the artichokes and leave them to drain, standing on their heads in a colander.

Artichoke, Chinese
Chinese artichokes (known in France as *crosnes*) are a most delicate and attractive vegetable with a convoluted appearance. These small, long-shaped white tubers are at their best cooked, unpeeled, in lightly salted water. They can then be: (1) dressed with a lemon-butter sauce; (2) sautéed with finely chopped ginger, garlic, lemon grass and fresh coriander; (3) tossed in a light soy-flavoured cream sauce; or (4) puréed with double cream and vegetable stock as a deliciously flavoured soup.

Artichoke, Jerusalem
The Jerusalem artichoke (similar in flavour to the Chinese artichoke) is a vegetable that was very popular in the nineteenth century. Its creamy-coloured to white flesh is slightly translucent, and very crisp when raw. Peel the long thin tubers with their knobby protusions and dip them immediately in acidulated water (as you would apples or pears) to preserve the colour. Or, more simply, cook them in their skins and peel them afterwards.

Cook and serve Jerusalem artichokes in the same manner as Chinese artichokes (see above). They are also good thinly sliced, dipped in a light batter and deep-fried.

Asparagus
Asparagus is one of those splendid vegetables which are almost invariably served as a separate course. It has a built-in sense of luxury and high living, and, although simple to cook, deserves care and a sense of occasion.

Before asparagus was widely used as a food, it enjoyed a great reputation as a medicine for almost everything from toothache to heart trouble. The early Greeks and Romans enjoyed this delicious vegetable both fresh, as we do, and dried. The dried stalks were prepared by boiling them, making them perhaps the first dehydrated vegetable.

Today, many varieties are available in this country: French asparagus, of which the best known and most delicious is the Argenteuil variety, Italian asparagus or purple Genoa asparagus, Belgian asparagus, German asparagus and, finally, green asparagus, which is subdivided into two types, small, used for garnishes and known as asparagus tips, and large, which is prepared much like Argenteuil asparagus.

I like to serve asparagus hot with melted butter and lemon juice or hollandaise sauce or cold with a *sauce ravigote* or vinaigrette. Asparagus tips make a delicious garnish and puréed asparagus make a delicious soup.

To prepare asparagus:
Wash the stalks thoroughly and, if sandy, scrub them gently with a vegetable brush. If there are some isolated leaf points below the head, remove them. To remove the woody base, break the stalks instead of cutting them. You will find that the stalk snaps off easily at the point where the tender part begins. Put the stalks in cold water as you clean and trim them.

To cook asparagus:
I find it best to sort home-grown asparagus into bundles of corresponding thickness, so that you can remove the thinner ones, as they will be ready before the thicker ends. Commercial bundles are usually graded to size already. Tie the bundles in two places.

To boil:
Select a deep, narrow saucepan in which the asparagus stalks can stand upright, and pour in boiling water to just under the tips (in this way the stalks can cook in water and the tender heads can cook in steam). Simmer gently; about 10 to 15 minutes from the time the water comes to the boil again after immersion is just about right.

To steam:
Lay the asparagus stalks flat in a gratin dish, add 4 tablespoons vegetable stock or water and 4 tablespoons butter and season with salt and freshly ground pepper, to taste. Place the gratin dish in the top of a double steamer over boiling water (or on a trivet or brick to hold the gratin dish over water in a large saucepan), cover, and steam for 15–20 minutes or until tender.

Aubergine

Carried into the Mediterranean area by Arabs in the early Middle Ages, the aubergine was a favourite with Greek, Turkish, Italian, French and Spanish cooks as far back as the twelfth century.

The Arabs used to scorch aubergines over charcoal, purée the creamy white flesh of the vegetable, season it with spices and garnish it with sesame and pomegranate seeds. The Turks, Greeks and Armenians combine the aubergine in many recipes with tomatoes, onion and herbs, the most prized dish being Imam Bayeldi (see page 107).

The aubergine has had a colourful career. At one time, it was thought that eating this exotic vegetable would cause insanity. Others damned it for its supposed aphrodisiac qualities. Today, we know the aubergine in Britain in two forms, egg-shaped and long-fruited, but in other parts of the world it is white, ash-coloured or brown, as well as the more familiar purple.

Do not peel aubergines. The skin contains a good deal of flavour and helps to hold the delicate flesh together in cooking.

Use aubergines, diced and sautéd in butter or olive oil, as an exotic garnish for any of the following dishes: scrambled eggs, poached eggs, omelettes, and as a savoury addition to vegetable casseroles.

Avocado Pears

Surprisingly enough, avocados have something of a reputation of being an acquired taste, so don't waste an avocado on someone unless you're sure that they'll like it.

Avocados vary considerably in size, from huge, pear-shaped fruit to little ones weighing no more than a few ounces. The skin can be smooth or slightly rough and the colour a bright green or deep violet.

Pick fruit which are heavy for their size and fairly firm, with just a hint of softness when pressed lightly with a finger. If they are too hard, leave for a day or two at normal room temperature. Never try to 'ripen' an avocado in the refrigerator.

To serve an avocado pear:
The traditional way of serving an avocado is to slice it in half, remove the stone (which comes out easily enough if the fruit is ripe) and replace it with a vinaigrette dressing.

Another favourite way is to scoop out some of the flesh, dice it and combine it with a little finely chopped onion, ketchup, and a vinaigrette dressing, or a little well-flavoured mayonnaise. Serve piled up in the half shell.

Whichever way you choose, make a point of protecting the flesh from discoloration by brushing it with lemon juice (or spooning over some of the vinaigrette you are going to serve) as soon as you cut it.

Beans, Green
French beans, *haricots verts*, string beans, just plain green beans, whatever you choose to call them, they are fabulous fare. They are at their very best and unfortunately most expensive in the markets when they are at their smallest and still stringless. All that needs to be done before cooking is to 'top and tail' them, wash them and place them in a bowl with a little butter and salt and freshly ground pepper. Then steam them over water or cook them in boiling salted water until they are tender. When they are a little older, it is necessary to remove the filament or 'string' that binds the two shells together. When they are older still (runner bean size), it is best to cut them diagonally in thin slices before cooking them as above.

Green beans should never be overcooked. For the ultimate in flavour, they should remain a little firm to the bite, *al dente* like Italian spaghetti or rice.

Green beans can be cooked in any number of ways. I like to serve them *au beurre* – cooked in boiling salted water until just tender, drained, cooled and then sautéd in butter just before serving with a pinch of finely chopped garlic or onion and 1 tablespoon chopped flat-leafed parsley. Another favourite way is *au béchamel*: boil the beans in boiling salted water until just tender, drain and then stir in béchamel sauce and sprinkle with finely chopped parsley.

Beetroot
Beetroot, as we know it today, was introduced to Northern Europe in the sixteenth century. Colours may vary from extremely dark red (almost purple) to bright red and down the scale to off-white.

When you buy beetroots ready cooked, select those with a deep red colour. If they are to be cooked at home, choose beetroots with a sound skin and be sure that this is not pierced or damaged in any way before cooking. Colour is very easily lost if water is allowed to penetrate the skin when cooking. For this reason, many cooks bake beetroot instead of boiling it.

Use beetroot simmered in vegetable stock as the foundation for a delicious soup. The beetroot is puréed with the stock and double cream after cooking.

Serve sliced cooked beetroot with a lemon sauce slightly thickened with cornflour, use sliced beetroot as a garnish for green salads, potato salads and apple and walnut salads dressed with mayonnaise. Dice cooked beetroot and combine with diced cooked potatoes, diced cooked turnips and diced cooked carrots for an interesting supper or luncheon salad.

Broccoli

Broccoli and its Italian cousin, the more highly flavoured calabrese, are vegetable favourites of mine. Both varieties are noted for their fine delicate flavour (the calabrese a little more bitter than the broccoli).

I like to separate broccoli into florets (reserving the tougher stems for another use, for example, in soup stocks or, thinly sliced, blanched and dipped in batter before deep-frying). I once served the stems as an interesting first course, blanched, simmered until tender in butter and soy sauce, turned into individual heatproof porcelain egg dishes, covered with a rich hollandaise sauce and put under the grill to brown just before serving.

To cook the broccoli florets, boil them until *al dente* in lightly salted water and serve them with melted butter flavoured with a little salt and lemon juice. Or blanch them and dip them in batter before deep-frying. In either case, do not overcook the delicate florets because, like asparagus, the heads are more tender than the stalks. If overcooked, they lose their attractive shape and become mushy.

Combine the lightly cooked florets with cooked spring vegetables – carrot and turnip chunks, tiny new potatoes and green peas – for a colourful vegetable medley; serve the same combination of vegetables cold with a well-flavoured vinaigrette. Make a pale green-tinted soup of the florets puréed with vegetable stock and double cream. Forget it, George Bush, this vegetable is supreme!

Brussels Sprouts

One of the most maligned of our winter vegetables is the common or garden 'sprout', usually served boiled with a pat of butter or margarine, gently swimming in its own water, almost invariably overcooked, and often – because of its advanced age – a trifle bitter to the taste. On festive occasions a few boiled chestnuts are added to this sorry dish.

Yet how different this misunderstood vegetable can be when treated with a little care and discrimination. Granted sprouts must first be boiled or steamed, but they should be cooked only until the very moment of tenderness if the delicate fresh flavour is to be preserved.

Brussels sprouts lend themselves happily to a multitude of variations. (1) Cook them in boiling salted water until just tender, not soft, then simmer them in butter with toasted breadcrumbs, a hint of garlic and a flavouring of lemon. (2) Toss the lightly cooked sprouts in butter or oil in a frying-pan and, just before serving, sprinkle with 4 tablespoons diced sautéed red pepper and chopped flat-leaved parsley. (3) Simmer the cooked sprouts in butter with 4 tablespoons slivered almonds and, just before serving, sprinkle with lemon juice and finely chopped flat-leafed parsley. (4) Simmer the cooked sprouts in butter, then moisten with sour cream.

Cabbage

The ancient Greeks served cabbage with rich savoury stuffings of meat and rice, flavoured with pine-nuts, currants, grated lemon peel and herbs. A vegetarian version transmutes this old favourite into subtle greatness by substituting diced red pepper, diced aubergine and diced courgette for the meat. Sour cabbage, known throughout the world today as sauerkraut, was an early Chinese invention. The Poles serve braised cabbage leaves deliciously stuffed with finely chopped onions, breadcrumbs, tomatoes and herbs. The Russians immortalize it in a superb peasant soup called *stchi*. The Austrians even make it into a sweet – cabbage strudel.

There are three main types of cabbage:
Green: The common or green cabbage, sold everywhere, is bright green in the summer months, whiter, firmer and larger in winter. The Savoy cabbage, bright deep green in colour with a curly leaf, is much more delicate in flavour. I like to use its tender leaves for stuffed cabbage recipes.
White: White cabbage is used commercially for the preparation of sauerkraut and is also used extensively for salads and coleslaw.
Red: Red cabbage is delicious, both raw and cooked. Always add lemon juice or vinegar to the water when cooking this attractive vegetable or it will turn purple in cooking. Red cabbage must be firm and the outer leaves bright in colour. Cut the head in quarters and remove the heavy veins, then shred the rest of the cabbage on a coarse shredder. Often served raw as an hors d'œuvre salad in France, red cabbage is equally delicious when shredded in this way, drained to the last drop of water in which it was cooked and then simmered gently in butter with diced apples and spices. A wonderful accompaniment to all grilled or poached vegetables.

Carrots

Particularly valuable for flavouring purposes in soups and stews, the carrot is a favourite standby (because of its bright colour, pleasing shape and delicate flavour) as a vegetable on its own. Ask anyone to name the most popular vegetables and you will find the versatile carrot high on the list. Rich in both starch and sugar, carrots (generally those with a deep orange colour) are rich in carotene (pro vitamin A) and contain many valuable mineral salts.

New carrots, so delicate that there is no suspicion of a woody core, so tender that a few minutes of gentle simmering in butter is all that is necessary to make them delicious, are best for serving as a vegetable. But the older ones, if carefully cooked to soften their somewhat woody fibre, can be used as the base for many delicious dishes or as a prime flavourer for stocks, soups and stews.

To prepare carrots:
Clean carrots with a stiff vegetable brush or with a stainless steel sponge. Do not peel them unless it is absolutely necessary, as there is so much goodness in and just under the skin. If you do not have to peel them, scrape them with a knife blade to remove only the smallest possible amount of skin.

Carrots may be diced, cubed, thinly sliced, diagonally sliced, cut into balls with a vegetable cutter, cut *en julienne* (matchstick-sized strips) or *en olives* (olive shapes).

Flavour carrots with butter, cream, sour cream, lemon juice, sherry, finely chopped parsley, dill or almonds.

To cook carrots:
There is no reason on earth to boil carrots in a pot full of water. I much prefer to blanch them (place the prepared carrots in a saucepan of cold water, bring to the boil and drain), then simmer them for 15–20 minutes in 4 tablespoons butter and 4 tablespoons vegetable stock, with sugar, salt and freshly ground pepper to taste. Delicious – even more so if you add 4 tablespoons double cream and a sprinkling of finely chopped parsley or fresh mint just before serving. Sour cream is good, too.

Cauliflower

The cauliflower – first cousin to the cabbage – is a much-maligned vegetable in this country. Usually boiled to a grey mush, it is then masked with white, cheese or parsley sauce. I far prefer this delicious vegetable (whole, or cut into florets) lightly steamed or simmered in salted water with a little lemon juice added until it is just tender, not mushy, then served with melted butter or any number of delicious sauces.

There are two basic methods of preparing cauliflower for the table, whole and in florets. In either case, never let the cauliflower become mushy. Undercook so that each separate segment keeps its identity, then mask it with a delicious sauce, and you will discover that it is one of your favourite vegetables.

To prepare cauliflower:
Trim the stem and remove outer green leaves from the cauliflower, then wash it and leave it for 30 minutes in cold salted water to which you have added a little lemon juice.

To cook cauliflower:
Whole cauliflower: Measure enough water to cover the cauliflower into a deep saucepan, add salt to taste, and bring to the boil. Put the cauliflower into the boiling water, bring to the boil again, then lower the heat, cover, and simmer gently for about 20 minutes or until the cauliflower is tender when pierced at the stem end with a fork. Do not overcook. Drain well, arrange on a heated serving dish, and top with melted butter or a sauce or garnish.
Cauliflorets: If you do not intend to cook the head whole, break or cut the cauliflower into florets. Prepare as for whole cauliflower, but cook for 10–15 minutes only so that the florets are tender but not mushy. Drain the florets and serve them with melted butter or a sauce or garnish.

Dress-ups for cauliflower
First prepare the cauliflower as above, either whole, or cut into florets.

Cauliflower hollandaise: Serve the hot cauliflower with a hollandaise sauce.

Cauliflower amandine: Sauté 4 tablespoons blanched slivered almonds in butter, pour over the hot cauliflower, and season to taste with salt and freshly ground pepper.

Cheesed cauliflower: Melt 4 tablespoons butter and add 4 tablespoons toasted breadcrumbs, ½ teaspoon grated onion, 4 tablespoons finely grated Gruyère cheese, 6 tablespoons crème fraîche, and season to taste with salt, freshly ground pepper and crushed dried chillies. Cook over a low heat, stirring constantly, until the cheese is melted, and pour over the cooked hot cauliflower.

Raw cauliflower: Eaten raw, cauliflower makes a most interesting appetizer or addition to a salad. Try raw cauliflorets mixed with other raw vegetables served with a spicy dip. Add a few tiny florets of raw cauliflower to a green salad for extra 'crunch' appeal. Or try the following: *Italian vegetable salad:* Chop and combine 4 peeled tomatoes, ½ peeled cucumber, ½ medium-sized red onion, 2 stalks of celery, and the florets from ½ raw cauliflower. Toss with Italian dressing (6 tablespoons olive oil, and 1–2 tablespoons balsamic vinegar, with salt, freshly ground pepper, crushed dried chillies and dried oregano to taste).

Celeriac

Celeriac, sometimes known as turnip-rooted celery, is available throughout most of the winter months. Its appearance is rather like a turnip but with a much rougher, yellowish-brown, pitted skin. When buying celeriac, make sure that the root is hard. If you pick up two of similar size, but of different weights, choose the heavier one, as the lighter one will not be in good condition. Celeriac can be stored in a cool, dry place for up to 2 weeks.

Celeriac can be eaten raw or lightly blanched as a delicious first-course salad when cut into thin strips and dressed with a vinaigrette or sour cream dressing or, more traditionally, with a mustard-flavoured mayonnaise thickened with sieved hard-boiled egg yolk. Try celeriac, too, as a vegetable – boiled or steamed, and dressed just before serving with a rich cream, hollandaise or mustard sauce. Celeriac, boiled with equal quantities of potato, puréed with double cream and butter, makes an excellent winter vegetable dish, especially when flavoured with freshly grated nutmeg or crushed coriander seeds.

Celery

One of the most useful vegetables I know, celery is perhaps at its best eaten raw – as a canapé filled with mashed Roquefort cheese, or as a refreshing hors d'œuvre on its own when dressed with a garlic- and fresh-herb-spiked vinaigrette dressing. When it is moist and crisp after the first touch of frost it is a deliciously fresh accompaniment to sliced cheese.

In its cooked state, celery is more often than not used as a flavouring agent, but it is delicious served on its own as a cooked vegetable topped with a rich cream or hollandaise sauce, or in a vegetable casserole. The green tops and coarser outside stalks are best for flavouring purposes, the crisp white inside stalks for serving raw.

Raw celery is low in calories since it consists primarily of water, and is therefore a frequent food in slimming diets. It is often recommended for rheumatism, and can be kept fresh for several days if the stalks are placed in a deep jug of cold water.

Chicory

Chicory (or Belgian endive, as it is often known in this country) can be eaten raw in salads, used as a handy base for canapés, or dressed with hot dressings as an interesting first course. *A word of warning:* the raw leaves tend to become easily discoloured after washing, unless kept wrapped in a cool place.

For raw chicory at its best, slice it into rings and blend with its dressing just before bringing it to the table. I like to serve it with clean-cut orange segments, dressed with a vinaigrette or a saffron- or tomato-flavoured mayonnaise dressing. Perfect when sprinkled with finely grated orange peel and a touch of finely chopped watercress leaves and garlic.

The slender, tender chicory root, with its highly edible white leaves, becomes a splendid dish when cooked. Try it braised with vegetable stock and finely chopped onion with a hint of lemon juice and sugar, or as the base for a delicious creamed soup when puréed with a little vegetable stock and double cream and thickened with egg yolks and lemon juice, much like a Greek garlic and lemon soup.

I first met chicory as it should be cooked in France (where to confuse the issue it is called endive), at a little quayside restaurant in Villefranche. The chicory, served as a separate course, was simmered gently in a small iron cocotte in a mixture of butter and oil with a splash of dry white wine. It was lightly seasoned with salt and freshly ground pepper, and no fewer than 5 sprigs of dried thyme and 5 fat cloves of garlic perfumed the whole. At first glance, too much of a good thing; but on tasting, perfection. Ever since then I have braised my chicory in the same way – sometimes with garlic and thyme, at others, for a subtler flavour, with the juice of orange or lemon. The lesson to be learned is that chicory and water do not mix as well as chicory and butter or oil.

Chicory has a delicate, bitter-sweet flavour that seems to demand intensification. I like to add one or more of the following: herbs, finely chopped onion, garlic, lemon juice, orange juice, dry white wine, béchamel, mornay or vinaigrette sauce. Chicory can also be puréed, to serve as a vegetable, a soup, or a soufflé. If it is too bitter, add a little sugar to the pan juices.

Courgettes

Courgettes – once so hard to come by in any except the more exotic food departments of the major stores and a few adventurous greengrocers – are now available in regular supplies in supermarkets throughout the country. Try this delicate, smooth-textured vegetable in any one of the following ways as an interesting first course, or as a separate vegetable course on its own.

Courgette 'coins': Slice the courgettes thinly, and simmer in butter or olive oil with ¼ crumbled vegetable stock cube and salt, freshly ground pepper and crushed dried chillies to taste, stirring constantly, until the courgettes are tender but still crisp and green. Serve immediately

Fried courgettes: Slice the courgettes thickly, or cut into thin strips about 5cm/2 inches in length. Roll in seasoned sifted flour and deep-fry in hot oil until golden. Serve immediately

Courgette Appetizer: Combine 2 tablespoons each of finely chopped onion, garlic and butter with 125ml/¼ pint each of dry white wine and water. Add 2 crushed garlic cloves and 1 bouquet garni (2 sprigs parsley, 1 sprig thyme, 1 bay leaf), and simmer for 10 minutes. Add the sliced courgettes and simmer until just tender. Transfer the courgettes to an earthenware dish, pour over the pan juices, chill and serve, garnished with chopped flat-leafed parsley or fresh coriander.

Cucumbers

Cooked cucumbers make a deliciously light vegetable dish. Peel the cucumbers and cut the flesh into thick short strips or into elongated olive shapes; parboil them for 3 minutes in boiling salted water, drain and then simmer them for a few minutes in a well-flavoured vegetable velouté (vegetable stock made with a cube and thickened with a roux of flour and butter) until tender. Garnish the dish with chopped flat-leafed parsley or fresh coriander, or diced red or yellow pepper, or finely chopped garlic and grated lemon peel.

Raw cucumbers, cut into thick rounds and hollowed out to make edible canapé cups, are delicious filled with (1) mashed avocado pear, seasoned with lemon juice, salt, freshly ground pepper, freshly grated onion and a little Mexican chile powder or crushed dried chillies; (2) a mixture of cream cheese, sour cream and finely diced red pepper, and topped with a larger dice of red pepper; (3) cold mashed potato, seasoned with a little finely chopped garlic, lemon juice, olive oil and salt, freshly ground pepper and crushed dried chillies to taste, and garnished with finely chopped (or sliced) red radish.

Thinly sliced raw cucumber, topped with a sour cream dressing flavoured with a little freshly grated onion and ginger and garnished with finely chopped parsley, tarragon or chives, makes an excellent cold hors d'œuvre. Or try paper-thin slices of raw cucumber, marinated in salt in the Danish manner until they are soft. Rinse and press dry; flavour with a light vinaigrette and use them to fill hollowed-out tomato cases.

Green Peas

Green peas, like so many good things came to us from France. There was no hint of peas other than dried in Britain until after the Norman Conquest. Then in the twelfth century 'green peas for Lent' were mentioned – proof that we had begun to take this delicious vegetable seriously at long last.

Fresh green peas – *petits pois à la Française* – suddenly became the rage of Paris in 1696: it was the custom to lick the freshly cooked peas from their shells after they had been dipped in a rich sauce. It became a fad, a craze, high fashion. "Some ladies, even after having supped at the Royal Table, and well supped, too," wrote Madame de Maintenon, favourite of Louis XIV, in that year, "return to their homes and at the risk of suffering from indigestion eat peas again before going to bed."

Young garden peas in the French seventeenth-century manner are still a firm favourite in Denmark today. Cook them in the pod for 10–15 minutes, until just tender, and then serve with herb-flavoured melted butter. Great fun to eat: just dip the pod into the butter, put it into your mouth holding the stem end with your fingers, then pull it out slowly with your teeth nearly closed, squeezing the peas into your mouth.

Use peas, both fresh and frozen, in a variety of ways to lend colour and interest to meals. Fresh pea soup, made from puréed peas, vegetable stock and cream, makes a flavoursome first course served hot with croûtons or chilled with finely chopped fresh mint or chives. A purée of fresh peas makes a refreshing change from that old standby, potatoes, as a brightly coloured accompaniment to a casserole of mixed vegetables. Or try a combination of peas, glazed carrots and button onions, piled into individual baked pastry cases, as a vegetable conversation piece.

To cook peas:
The old-fashioned method of boiling peas in a saucepan of water and then throwing the water away has much to condemn it. So many of the valuable vitamins and trace elements are lost in the water, and the peas themselves lose so much of their flavour and identity. I much prefer to steam fresh peas to obtain the utmost in flavour, or to cook them in heavy, shallow saucepans with tight-fitting lids for almost waterless cooking, with just a little vegetable stock or water and a little butter to add lustre and savour. When served hot with butter and salt and freshly ground pepper or with a few tablespoons of vegetable velouté sauce, they become food fit for the gods.

Always serve peas as soon as possible after cooking, as they tend to lose flavour and texture if kept warm over any period of time.

Leeks
The leek, first cousin to garlic and a well-known member of the onion tribe, is one of the simplest and homeliest of all winter vegetables. Known lovingly to the French as 'poor man's asparagus', the leek, nonetheless, lends its fine savour and earthy authority to many great French delicacies whose fame has travelled the world.

I like to combine leeks with onions and garlic as an aromatic threesome for the great French soups or a pot-au-feu of vegetables. Simmer baby leek segments gently with carrots and potatoes cut to the same size and serve with a mustard and cream sauce. Purée the leeks with cream, vegetable stock and potatoes to make one of the finest cold soups in the world, vichyssoise. Try leeks on their own, puréed with vegetable stock and cream, for a delicious cream of leek soup. Serve this versatile vegetable in a variety of ways: leeks *à la Grèque* (leeks simmered in dry white wine and olive oil with finely chopped onions and carrots), Leeks *à la vinaigrette* (leeks poached in water and served with a vinaigrette sauce), leeks *au gratin* (leeks baked in a cream sauce), and leeks mornay (poached leeks served with a well-flavoured cheese sauce).

To prepare leeks:
While leeks may be one of the mildest flavoured members of the onion family, they are also apt to be one of the earthiest when freshly picked. To ensure that the leeks are not gritty with sand or soil, trim off the roots and cut of the tops, leaving 2.5–7cm/1–3 inches of the green portion. Halve the leeks, leaving the halves attached at the root end, and wash carefully.

To boil leeks:
Clean and trim the leeks as above and simmer in boiling salted water for 20 minutes or until tender. Drain thoroughly. Sprinkle with finely chopped parsley and serve with melted butter.

Mushrooms
The Greeks claimed that mushrooms were the food of the gods; not surprisingly, for they are one of the most delicious of vegetables. Rich in phosphoric acid and albuminoids –

on a nutritional level with lean beef – they are a nourishing food on their own.

There is, of course, small comparison between a wild mushroom and a cultivated one. To the true mushroom enthusiast, one morel, one chanterelle or girolle, is worth fifty of the commercial variety. But for the average city-dweller, unable to pick his own, the cultivated mushroom adds much to the savour of good cooking.

There are many uses for the mushroom other than as a seasoning ingredient for casseroles, soups, stews and gravies. Besides the more usual mushroom soufflés, sauces and stuffings, I like to make a salad of raw mushrooms, a soup in which the mushrooms are sieved raw into the stock and just simmered gently for 5 minutes to keep their fresh-tasting flavour, and large mushroom caps stuffed with marinated crisp vegetables for a refreshing summer starter.

Mushrooms last longer and better when kept in the refrigerator, but should in any case be used within 2 or 3 days of purchase. Don't bother to peel fresh mushrooms. Just cut off the tips of the stalks and wipe with a damp cloth, or wash quickly in cold water and dry thoroughly.

Use both caps and stalks in cooking unless the recipe states caps only. In this case, save the stalks for flavouring casseroles, stews and gravies.

Don't overcook fresh mushrooms. They are naturally tender. I prefer to sauté them in butter, or butter and lemon juice, for 5–6 minutes only.

Mushrooms vary in size from 2.5cm/1 inch buttons to 7–10cm/3-4 inches across. Tinned mushrooms can be substituted for fresh ones in many recipes. Dried mushrooms are used for many Continental dishes.

Okra

Okra (sometimes known as ladies' fingers or bamia) is grown extensively in India, Africa and the Middle East, in the warmer parts of North and South America and in the West Indies. Sold in this country in Greek, Middle Eastern and Indian shops, it is available all year round. When overcooked, the flesh of the Okra becomes very glutinous, and it is used in Greek recipes as a thickening agent for casseroles and stews. I much prefer it cooked in lightly salted water for 3–4 minutes only, when it keeps its crisp flavourful appearance to be served with a spicy tomato-based dip as a light appetizer. I also like it, prepared in this way, added to cooked vegetable dishes such as tomatoes, courgettes and aubergines, or flavoured with curry spices to accompany Indian foods.

Onions

The onion, the oldest known vegetable in the world, was among the foodstuffs which fed the Egyptian workmen building the pyramids. Today, this versatile vegetable is served fried, sautéd, boiled, baked, creamed and stuffed.

I used to love the great sandwiches of fried onions and red peppers and sliced hard-boiled eggs we enjoyed in America when I was young. Made of slices of toasted bread with this hot, savoury mixture inside, they were almost a meal in themselves. And in the summer there were fresh tasting salads – red, green and white – containing sliced onion rings, tomatoes and green peppers.

Onions and carrots, glazed in a little vegetable stock, butter and sugar combine to make a perfect accompaniment to baked pumpkin, butternut pumpkin or sweet potatoes in a cream sauce. And make onion and potato gratin, a dish from Northern France. You will find it a wonderful change from the usual puréed potatoes with your Sunday lunch. Creamy and rich, with a crusty top, it is a welcome addition to the winter vegetable scene.

A little finely chopped onion, a tablespoon or two, no more, browned in butter with a little finely chopped parsley and a hint of garlic adds greatly to the savour of grilled vegetables. Add a whole onion, stuck with a pungent clove or two, to a hot-pot of winter vegetables. Serve a dish of creamed onions as an intriguing first course on their own. Accompany the onions with freshly grated Parmesan, much as you would pasta. If the onions are small enough, present them in a baked pastry case for added effect.

The larger onions imported from Spain and Portugal are much milder in flavour than our own and are more suitable for serving as a vegetable. If your onions tend to be strong in flavour, scald them in boiling water before cooking them.

Cooking in water or in the oven always softens the onion's harmful esters and renders it sweet. Blanch spring onions (those with large heads) – they make wonderful vegetable accents for spinach when combined with sautéd red and yellow pepper strips.

Parsnips
Parsnips resemble young carrots in appearance although they are much lighter in colour. Rich in sugars and starch, the parsnip has a very special 'parsnippy' flavour of its own: sweet and slightly nutty. At their best, like celery, after frost, parsnips make an excellent flavouring vegetable for vegetable stocks, soups and winter casseroles. But they really come into their own when served simply boiled and tossed in butter and lemon juice with a hint of crushed coriander seed or nutmeg. I like to use them, too, thinly sliced as a delicious gratin (such as French Potato and Turnip Gratin, p. 161).

Parsnips and carrots, cut into thin strips and baked in a foil parcel, are delicious when a tablespoon of chilled herb and garlic butter is included in each foil packet before baking. The packets – like foil-wrapped medium -sized potatoes – should be baked for 45 minutes in a moderate oven.

Peppers
South American Indians began eating wild peppers called chillies 5–6,000 years before Christ. Brought back to Europe by the first *conquistadores* in both its wild and its cultivated state, the chilli pepper was the principal seasoning agent first of the Incas and then of the Aztecs. From Mexico City, the love of this fiery seasoning agent spread northwards to south-western America, where it became a firm favourite with the Pueblo Indians who include it in their recipes today.

We have Christopher Columbus to thank for the pepper. A long, green, spicy vegetable in its native state, it was called *aji* by the Mayan natives until the Spanish gave their own word *pimiento* to it when they brought back the seeds to Spain.

The pepper family, as we know it today, is vast and varied. Peppers come in hundreds of types, from the sweetest-tasting to the hottest, from green to yellow to fiery red, or a mixture of all three. Many cooks are wary of buying red peppers. They think that all red types are hot. This is not so: a red pepper may be hot or mild, depending on the variety. It is useful to know that the 'sweet' green pepper ripens through yellow to brilliant red, but these most colourful versions are actually mellower and sweeter than the green and a little less tough in texture.

Peppers are one of the mildest and most easily digested of all vegetables if the tough outer skin is charred black and rubbed off. Use roasted peppers as main dishes, as containers for rice and mixed vegetables, and as vegetable garnishes.

Red or yellow peppers may be substituted for green peppers in any of the following recipes. Served cold, side by side on a bed of lettuce, or hot in a rich tomato sauce, they make a festive dish.

Serve peppers as a main course, as an accompaniment to roast and grilled vegetables and as a vegetable garnish. The possible variations depend only on your own ingenuity and imagination. Crisp green and yellow pepper rings, dressed with olive oil and lime juice, make a wonderful salad; alternatively, 1 small green pepper, seeded and finely chopped, can be combined with peeled, seeded and finely chopped tomatoes and a little finely chopped onion for a novel salad dressing. This is particularly good with a salad of sliced, poached courgettes (or peeled poached slices of marrow) and lettuce leaves.

Sautéed pepper strips make a delicious garnish for main dishes of baked or grilled vegetables. Choose firm, fresh peppers – 1 per person – and wash and seed them. Cut them into strips and sauté them gently in hot olive oil and butter until just tender, then season to taste with salt, freshly ground pepper and a dash of lemon juice.

Plantains

Plantains resemble extra large, rough-skinned bananas, but are used in vegetarian recipes more like a potato or sweet potato. To peel them, blanch whole plantains in boiling water for 2–3 minutes, remove from the water, score the skin from the top to bottom with a sharp knife, and gently prise away the skin.

Deep fry thin rounds of plantain to make delicious chips; sauté them in butter or oil with a little crumbled vegetable stock cube for added flavour; cut blanched plantain into slices 5cm/2 inches thick; sprinkle them with lemon juice and crumbled vegetable stock cube and roast them in oil or butter in a preheated oven until tender; or dip blanched slices in a curry-flavoured batter and deep-fry until the *beignet* casing is crisp and golden. Delicious served with a savoury sauce.

Potatoes

The potato is undoubtedly the world's number one vegetable. Yet its almost universal acceptance today dates only from the seventeenth and eighteenth centuries. Sir John Hawkins gets the credit for introducing the potato into Ireland in 1565, Sir Walter Raleigh planted it there in 1585 … but it was not until the mid-nineteenth century that the potato became the important staple crop that it is today in Northern Europe, the British Isles and North America.

There are hundreds of ways of preparing potatoes. Some of the simplest are the best. Baked in the oven and rushed to the table, where they are quickly slashed open to receive a pat of butter and a sprinkling of coarse salt and freshly ground pepper, or puréed with double cream and butter, or crisp fried in hot oil, they are hard to beat. I like, too, to serve new potatoes no bigger than walnuts, hot and dry in their jackets with lashings of butter and salt and freshly ground pepper. Or try the more sophisticated *gratin dauphinois* (new potatoes, peeled and thinly sliced, cooked in the oven with double cream and freshly grated Gruyère and Parmesan cheeses), or *pommes de terre Anna* (new potatoes, peeled and thinly sliced, arranged in concentric layers in a well-buttered, thick casserole, each layer brushed with butter, and baked in the oven until a crisp golden crust has formed).

I like, too, the hash browned potatoes of my youth. The potatoes, first boiled in their jackets, were then peeled and coarsely chopped before being browned in a heavy iron frying pan in equal quantities of butter and olive oil. The potatoes were pressed down into the pan and cooked slowly until brown – it was always necessary to turn them once or twice at the beginning to make sure that some of the crusty brown bits got into the interior of the potato cake. The entire bottom of the cake was then allowed to brown before the potatoes were turned over with a spatula, like an omelette, to brown on the other side.

Choose potatoes best suited to your purpose. Baking potatoes are large, with a fine, mealy texture when cooked. Use them for baking and for soups and purées. New potatoes range in size from tiny ones no bigger than a walnut to those the size of a regular potato. Serve small new potatoes cooked in their jackets as above, or peeled and simmered gently in butter and lemon juice until tender. Use larger ones for potato salads and for cooked dishes such as *gratin dauphinois*, for which you want potato slices to keep their shape. Never bake a new potato.

Whenever possible, cook potatoes in their jackets. Most of the food value of the potato lies just under the skin and is lost if it is peeled away. If you prefer serving them without their jackets, the skins will slip off easily enough after cooking. If you peel raw potatoes, put them into a bowl of cold water immediately to prevent them changing colour.

Do not overcook potatoes. Test them with a fork – they are done when you can pierce them easily. Never allow them to become watery and mushy.

Pumpkins

Pumpkins are large, orange-skinned vegetables that seem to spell autumn menus. Under-used by cooks in this country, perhaps because of their great size (a large pumpkin can weigh up to 39.37kg/100lb), they can be bought by the slice or by the pound for the adventurous vegetarian cook. A more recent arrival on the pumpkin scene is the small individual pumpkin, used mainly for decoration during the autumn months. But these little pumpkins make delicious individual servings of pumpkin soup when the diced flesh is simmered with chopped onions and aromatics in vegetable stock and cream to make creamed pumpkin soup served in its own little pumpkin shell, lightly roasted in the oven to warm it through just before serving.

I like pumpkins, too, cut into golden cubes, pan-fried or oven-roasted until tender in butter and olive oil, then served with a creamed or curried sauce; or as the orange-tinted base for a colourful topping of stir-fried cubed vegetables in a Thai sauce. For an unusual starter, try the Pumpkin Terrine recipe (page 74) with its easy-to-make ivory sauce.

Spinach

'Vegetables in England are served in all the simplicity of nature, like hay to horses, only a little boiled instead of dried.'

This was the comment of some unknown disenchanted visitor to these isles. For vegetables are our weak spot, all the world acknowledges that, and it is not the elaborate dishes that trip us up. It is in the simplest methods that we fail.

Take spinach, for example. An exotic from Persia, it was brought by the Moors to Spain, by the Spaniards to the Low Countries, by Flemish refugees to England. And after that great pilgrimage, we plunge it into cold water, boil it and force it on our children.

To prepare fresh spinach:
Because of its high water content, spinach should be cooked only in the water that clings to its leaves after washing. Do not boil it in water. For a really superb flavour, add several tablespoons fresh butter, season with salt and freshly ground pepper to taste, and cook as in the basic recipe below.

It is necessary to wash spinach well in several changes of cold water, at the same time removing any possible sand or grit and all yellowed or damaged leaves and tough stalks.

To cook fresh spinach:
Put 900g–1.35kg/2–3lb fresh washed and drained spinach leaves in a thick-bottomed saucepan with 4 tablespoons butter, and salt and freshly ground pepper to taste. Simmer gently, stirring constantly, until the spinach is soft and tender. The mass of crisp leaves will begin to 'dissolve' almost at the first contact with the heat, and there will be just enough to serve 4–6 new spinach fanciers.

Swedes and Turnips
Swedes and turnips have their own flavours and their own colours and yet they are the same family of root vegetables, known to cooks since ancient times. Pliny, in the first century, described long tubular turnips and flat spheroid turnips as *napa* and *napus*. In Anglo-Saxon, the word became *naep*. Today, the vegetable is known as neeps, and bashed neeps is as popular in Scotland as a golden, scented accompaniment to haggis as it was all those centuries ago.

In Henry VIII's England, turnip and swede roots were boiled or baked, the tender tops cooked as greens and the tender young leaves used in 'sallets', much as we do today.

Serve tender young turnips in navarins of spring vegetables; add turnips to basic stocks and purée them with vegetable stock, cream and carrots for deliciously light cream soups. Or purée the young turnips, or fuller grown swedes, with butter and cream for a delicious vegetable. Young turnips are also good boiled or steamed and served with Old English egg or parsley sauce. For a more unusual touch, combine thinly sliced young turnips with chopped green tops and black-eyed beans for a rustic dish from America's deep south.

Use turnips and swedes, cut into thin strips, together with equal-sized carrot strips, for a glowingly coloured dish of mixed root vegetables. Delicious accompanied by hot vegetable cream sauce and chilled apple sauce flavoured with cinnamon and nutmeg.

Sweetcorn
What summer flavour treat can be compared to a steaming hot cob of golden sweetcorn, with a knob of fresh butter and a sprinkling of salt and crushed dried chillies in the plate to rub the corn in before each bite? This is finger food at its best!
Sweetcorn, once considered primarily as animal fodder in this country, is now a firm favourite on our shelves. Baby corn cobs, too, are readily available in greengrocers and supermarkets around the country. To cook sweetcorn, strip away the green outer husks and all the silky threads inside and wash under cold running water. Corn on the cob, as far as I am concerned, is best plain boiled in unsalted water.

To boil sweetcorn, put the prepared cobs of corn into a pan of boiling unsalted water and cook for 5–7 minutes if they are garden fresh, longer (up to 15 minutes) for older corn. Brush with melted butter and season with salt, freshly ground pepper and, for an authentic Mexican touch, crushed dried chillies.

To serve sweetcorn as an accompaniment to roast or grilled vegetables – or to include it in a vegetable casserole – it is usually better to strip the grains from the cob with a sharp knife. Use young, tender corn, just picked from the garden, raw in a salad with slivered raw cabbage, dried raisins and sliced apple in a sour cream and mayonnaise, or vinaigrette, dressing.

Sweet Potatoes

Exotic sweet potatoes deserve to be better known in this country. You will often find them in West Indian shops and street markets in the major cities as well as in supermarkets. The gnarled, orange-red, tubular roots can grow to an enormous size. Avoid the very big ones – they tend to be fibrous – and choose the small uniform ones just big enough for one person. I like them simply baked in the oven until cooked through, slit with a cross at the top, then pressed open and dressed for the table with a large knob of butter and a sprinkling of salt, freshly ground pepper and crushed dried chillies. Larger ones can be peeled, cut into thick slices, and baked in the oven with melted butter, a pinch or two of crumbled vegetable stock cube and a splash of orange or lemon juice to give them added flavour. Boiled sweet potatoes, whipped with double cream, butter and a hint of orange juice, brown sugar and freshly grated nutmeg, make a sweet potato mash to remember.

To boil sweet potatoes, scrub them and cut them into chunks that will fit easily into your saucepan. Fill the saucepan with salted water and bring to the boil. Add the sweet potatoes and cook for 15–20 minutes or until soft (test with the point of a knife as you would ordinary potatoes). Drain, peel and serve hot with butter, *crème fraîche* or sour cream, and the usual seasonings.

Tomatoes

In 1518 Cortés discovered a small tart red Mexican fruit – cousin of the deadly nightshade – that was to change the culinary history of the world. At first the *tomatl*, as it was called by the Aztecs, met with little favour in Spain; it was considered too tart as a fruit to be anything more than a herbal curiosity.

Then an adventurous chef at the Spanish court tried combining it with onions, oil, vinegar and pepper and created the world's most popular sauce.

The fame of the tomato rapidly spread from Spain to Italy, where it was termed *pomo de' Mori*, or Moor's apple, and from there it was a quick jump to *pomodoro*, or golden apple, which remains the Italian word for the tomato today. The French, next in line to become interested in this fragrant fruit, called it *pomme d'amour*, or love apple, a nodding bow to its supposed aphrodisiac qualities and a corruption of the Italian term.

Today the tomato is one of the world's most popular fruits. More than 600 million pounds of fresh tomatoes are consumed every year in this country alone. That means over 6kg/13lb a head. The success story of the tomato is well deserved; its vivid colouring and sharp, sweet flavour make it a star attraction on any table.

I like to serve stuffed raw tomatoes as a cold first course for summer luncheons. Fill them with: (1) mashed flesh of avocado pear flavoured with salt, pepper, lemon and onion juice; (2) saffron rice, garnished with finely chopped olives, pimento and onions and dressed with a vinaigrette dressing; or (3) diced yellow peppers, cucumbers and black olives in a rémoulade sauce.

Stuffed tomatoes Provençal make a delicious hot luncheon dish which literally breathes South of France.

Italian tomato sauce is always a standby in my kitchen. It will keep for a week in the refrigerator. Use its sharp authority for pasta, for grilled vegetables, and as a base for Italian devilled eggs. This light luncheon dish (poached eggs in tomato sauce) is usually served in individual fireproof ramekins.

Watercress

One of the most delicious vegetable dishes I know is the fresh-tasting green purée of watercress served at one of France's greatest restaurants, the Pyramide at Vienne. A creation of the world-famous French chef Fernand Point, this dish makes the most of the tangy, peppery freshness of delicate watercress leaves, their sharpness and pungency smoothed with the addition of a little fresh cream, farmhouse butter and perhaps an egg yolk or two of. Its sharp green colour and distinctive flavour make watercress purée the perfect accompaniment to roast or grilled root vegetables.

Watercress – long acknowledged in this country as a welcome addition to the salad bowl and as an attractive, if ever-present, garnish for cooked dishes of all kinds – is beginning to come into its own as a salad in its own right and as a cooked vegetable. Raw, it contains appreciable quantities of iron, iodine, sulphur and vitamins A and C; cooked, it goes well with butter, fresh cream, gravy or a hollandaise sauce; puréed with the addition of fresh cream, butter, and potatoes to give it body, it makes an excellent vegetable or a wonderfully appetizing soup.

Raw watercress never tastes better than when combined in a salad with oranges and finely-sliced onion rings and served with a curry dressing. Or try teaming it with thinly sliced mushrooms or diced tomatoes, and serve with a well-flavoured vinaigrette dressing. Or dress a salad of chilled cooked vegetables with a well-flavoured vinaigrette to which you have added a handful of chopped watercress leaves. Sprinkle chopped watercress leaves, too, on cocktail canapés and cooked vegetables.

Watercress needs very little preparation. Trim the root ends; untie the bunches and carefully remove the roots and damaged or yellow leaves. Wash thoroughly under cold running water and drain. For a simple vegetable accompaniment, place washed water-cress sprigs in a large saucepan with just the water which clings to them, sprinkle with salt and 'melt' the watercress over a low heat, stirring gently, for about 5 minutes, or until the stems are tender but not soft; drain well and serve with melted butter or a hollandaise sauce. Watercress makes a delicious soup (for the simplest version combine it with potatoes, salt, lemon juice and butter); try it, too, in omelettes and as an unusual stuffing for vegetables.

Watercress sauce: One of the easiest cold sauces I know. Rub ½ bunch of fresh watercress through a fine sieve with 125ml/¼ pint well-flavoured mayonnaise and season to taste with 2 tablespoons tomato ketchup and a dash of Tabasco or Worcestershire sauce. Chill.

Watercress cheese: Blend 2 packets cream cheese with 4 tablespoons finely chopped watercress leaves.

Watercress cheese spread: Blend 1 packet cream cheese with ½ carton sour cream. Add 4 tablespoons finely chopped watercress leaves. Use as a fresh-tasting spread for cocktail canapés. Top with finely chopped radishes or a slice of hard-boiled egg or cucumber.

Spices

Allspice

Allspice is the dried, hard, unripe berry of the pimento or allspice tree, a member of the bay family. It was thought by Columbus to be the much sought-after 'pepper', and was brought back in great triumph to Europe. Often called the Jamaican pepper, it closely resembles the true pepper in shape, but has a delicately fragrant flavour - pungent and aromatic - that tastes like a blend of cinnamon, nutmeg and mace, strongly spiced with cloves. The French call this spice *quatre épices.*

Allspice is excellent for vegetable stuffings and vegetable sausage mixtures. Use allspice, ground or whole, in ragouts of vegetables and highly-flavoured sauces for exotic vegetables such as plantains, yams, sweet potatoes and pumpkin. Use it whole for pickles and marinades; add two or three of the pungent berries to a fresh pea soup, or to flavour chutneys, ketchup and spiced fruits. Use it with a light hand to flavour delicate sauces for eggs and poached vegetables and let its subtle fragrance accent hot puddings, fruit pies and ginger or marmalade flavoured cakes.

Aniseed

Strongly flavoured and highly scented if used too lavishly, aniseed has a subtle, wonderfully pleasant liquorice flavour when used with a light touch in cooking. Sometimes called sweet cumin, to which it has a slight similarity in flavour, it is used widely in confectionery and in cake and pastry-making. French cooks pound aniseed with lump sugar to flavour sponge cakes, custards or creams, sometimes adding a little anisette or Pernod to the blend for extra richness or flavour.

Aniseed is also distilled to make Pernod and anisette, two French liqueurs of distinction. I like to sprinkle aniseed on cakes and cookies, or on pre-baked pastry cases for custard cream tarts studded with peaches or pears. And use it, too, in the Oriental manner to add flavour and interest to delicate stir-fries of white vegetables.

Cardamom

Cardamom, which belongs to the ginger family, once had a reputation as an aphrodisiac and was consequently used by certain chefs of the French court for its reputedly 'warming' qualities. Cardamom has much of the same fire as ginger, allspice and black pepper, but with a decided spicy orange hint in its flavour. It is used in India as one of the prime ingredients of hot curry powders and sauces. I like to use this attractive pod with pink peppercorns and nutmeg and cloves to flavour pilaus of rice. Cardamom pods, lightly crushed with a little sugar, give a wonderfully different flavour to a vinaigrette dressing for a 'green salad' of sliced, peeled avocado and kiwi fruit. Try it to scent Indian teas and fruit ices or, in the Arabian manner, to spice hot coffee.

Chile powder

Chile powder is an American spice blend, now available in this country, and a necessary ingredient of the famous Mexican dishes Chile Beans and Chile con Carne. This fragrant dark-coloured spice blend (not in any way to be confused with powdered chillies) is a delicious combination of the finely ground pods of several different kinds of Mexican hot peppers blended with paprika, cumin seed, dried garlic and oregano. Its rich flavour and colour is used in Mexican and south-western American cooking as well as in tropical countries to flavour native dishes, sauces and soups. It is almost an essential in south-western and South American bean dishes.

Cinnamon

A spice highly prized by the ancients, cinnamon is made from the dried, spicy inner bark of the cinnamon tree, first cousin to the cassia and the bay tree. Its fragrant odour and sweet, spicy flavour is the perfect foil, when used in moderation, to bean and lentil dishes. Use it, like Arab cooks, in combination with ground ginger and cumin, paprika and powdered saffron to lend flavour and excitement to vegetable grills and casseroles. Add finely chopped coriander, garlic and onion and a little olive oil to this fragrant mix and you have *chermoula*, the famous Arabian 'dry' marinade used to flavour the ingredients for couscous.

Combine cinnamon with pepper, ginger, cloves and mace and use this mixture to rub on peeled root vegetables before baking in the oven. Add a hint of cinnamon and cloves to Dijon mustard to flavour thick 'steaks' of pumpkin, sweet potatoes and yams before baking or grilling.

Spice mulled wine with cinnamon. Let this spice add interest to sweets, cakes and puddings. Sprinkle it over coffee, sliced fresh fruits and creamed puddings. Its highly fragrant odour and sweet, aromatic flavour is a must for apple pies, dumplings, sauces and puddings.

Cloves

Cloves, like pepper, were one of the first oriental spices to excite the cupidity of Western spice traders. First used by the Chinese, the clove has a hot, spicy flavour and a highly aromatic scent. Use whole cloves for pickling, for fruit pies and sauces and for hot fruit compotes. Stick an onion with one or two cloves before adding it to a vegetable stew or casserole; use cloves (with finely chopped onions and garlic and soy) to add interest to oriental stir-frys of root vegetables. Use ground cloves in spice cakes, gingerbreads, puddings and sweets.

Coriander seed

Sweet, yet tart and lemony in flavour, coriander is a favourite ingredient of hot curries and sauces. I find that ground coriander is delicious when mixed with equal quantities of salt and pepper and rubbed on thick 'steaks' of root vegetables such as swedes, turnips, sweet potatoes and yams. Try this fragrant mix, too, with butternut pumpkin, pumpkin or bean soups and casseroles, and for aromatic, breadcrumb-based stuffings for roast onions, potatoes or pumpkin. Try this spice, too, coarsely ground, as a fragrant covering for soft cream cheeses, or whole in pickles; and use it sparingly, when finely ground, in puddings and pastries.

Cumin seed

Cumin is an essential ingredient of many Far Eastern and oriental recipes. Its strong, aromatic scent and pungent flavour (similar to caraway seed, but much stronger and more interesting in flavour) is used extensively in Mexican cookery, Indian curries and as a delicious 'flavourer' for vegetable 'meat' loaves and for anything made with dried beans or lentils. One of my favourite uses for whole cumin seeds is as an attractive 'wrapping' for cubes of cream cheese.

Curry powder

Commonly known as a spice, curry powder is actually a blend of many herbs and spices; commercial varieties may contain between eight and thirty different sorts. Connoisseurs who really appreciate curry have special formulas of freshly ground herbs and spices for various dishes. The following list (which reads like a complete herb and spice index) will give you some idea of the principal ingredients it is possible to include in a well-blended curry powder: allspice, aniseed, bay leaves, cardamom, cinnamon, cloves, coriander, cumin, dill, fennel, garlic, ginger, mace, mustard, nutmeg, black pepper, white pepper, red pepper, paprika, poppy seeds, saffron, turmeric. The relative strength of the blend, of course, depends on how much hot pepper and ginger is used.

Ginger

One of the earliest oriental spices to be known to Europe, ginger originally came from southern China, where the ripe roots were carefully selected, boiled in several waters to remove some of their fire, and then preserved in thick syrup. Use sliced preserved ginger in syrup to add interest to fruit salads and compotes, or to stud ginger cakes and ice creams. Chop the preserved ginger in syrup and use for an interesting sauce for cakes, sweets, creams, ice creams and puddings.

Ginger was used widely in the cuisines of the ancient Greeks and Romans and Arabs and is still used widely around the world today. It was used in India in early times and in Britain, where it is used to flavour apple sauces, chutneys and stewed fruits. I like to sprinkle honeydew melons with ginger and lime juice, and often use this pungent spice mixed with butter and cake crumbs as a comforting topping for cakes and custards.

This extremely pungent spice should be creamy white in colour when ground. It is shiny-skinned and light-buff in colour when whole. Whole fresh ginger is now very popular in this country and is still much used, finely chopped, in combination with finely chopped garlic and lemon grass, to season stir-fried or grilled dishes of all kinds. I suggest using this combination of pungent aromatics to flavour grills and stir-frys of mixed vegetables and to flavour bouillons for vegetable-based clear broths and vegetable soups.

Mace

Mace, the dried outer sheath of the kernel of the fruit of the nutmeg tree and similar, if more intense, in flavour, is an expensive spice (only 5g/¼ oz is obtained per 450g/1 lb of nutmeg harvested). I like to use a little ground mace for pickling, and to flavour marinades and sauces for winter vegetables. I use it with a lighter hand for cakes, sweets and puddings, but add it with impunity to any sweet where chocolate plays a leading part.

Try a hint of mace with hard-boiled eggs or vegetables in a rich cream sauce. It makes all the difference. Cauliflower and carrots, particularly, take kindly to a touch of mace, and pureed potatoes and sweet potatoes, even parsnips and yams, when enriched with cream and butter, are all the better for a dash of this versatile spice.

Mustard
Mustard was well known to the ancient Romans, who imported it into Gaul where it quickly found favour. The French moisten powdered white and black mustards with verjuice (to make Dijon mustard) or with wine (to make Bordeaux mustard) and add herbs for various special mustard blends. It is very hot in flavour. I like to use mustard to flavour cream and hollandaise sauces for poached vegetables and of course it is a 'must' for home-made mayonnaise. Use this hot spice in pickles, chutneys and relishes, and in salad dressings.

Nutmeg
Delicate and at the same time very aromatic, nutmeg is the dried seed of the fruit of the nutmeg tree. Usually used as a substitute for, or as an adjunct to the more expensive mace, this spice is very stimulating to the palate. I love freshly-ground nutmeg in creamy desserts like rice pudding; use it to give added flavour to couscous, kasha, quinoa and barley when served as vegetable accompaniments to grilled, roasted or casseroled vegetables. This pungent spice is a must for flavoured creamed sauces for vegetables. I have even been known to grind a little nutmeg into a creamed cheesy sauce for ribbon noodles.

Paprika
One of the spices the Turks brought with them to western Europe was paprika, or Turkish pepper as it was called in the sixteenth century - the same sweet red pepper or aji discovered by Columbus in the New World. Warmly aromatic and a rich red in colour, paprika is used a great deal in French, Spanish, Moroccan and Hungarian cooking. Use this mild, sweet cousin to the red pepper to add colour and flavour to creamed sauces for eggs and poached vegetables. Sprinkle it for a colourful accent on eggs mayonnaise, tomatoes mayonnaise or a Russian salad of mixed diced vegetables. I like to add paprika to cream soups and cooked cheese dishes of all kinds. A simple grilled cheddar toast for supper would not be the same without a light sprinkling of equal quantities of ground paprika, cayenne and sea salt: it makes all the difference. And of course it would be the prime ingredient of an Hungarian-inspired vegetarian dish of vegetables *paprikash* (vegetables simmered in oil and butter with finely-chopped onion and garlic and lashings of paprika). Try this same idea, too, with the addition of red peppers, for a warming goulash of winter vegetables.

Pepper
One of the prime motivating factors for Columbus's voyage to the Spice Islands, pepper is our most widely-used spice. Columbus found several kinds of pepper: the black seeds whose aroma was much like that of cloves, cinnamon and nutmeg (our famous allspice) called Jamaican pepper for centuries, and the spicy vegetable which the Mayan natives called *aji* (the red pepper family).

Black pepper: one of the first spices to be introduced to Europe, this is the dried, unripe fruit of *piper nigrum*, found in the East Indies. This spice lends flavour and excitement to most foods. It quickly loses flavour and aroma when ground. I prefer to grind it with a pepper mill as and when I use it.

White pepper: less pungent and less aromatic than black pepper, this is the same seed freed from its outer skin. It is perfect for lighter sauces, for mayonnaise, hollandaise and bearnaise, and in any light-coloured dish where specks of black pepper would be unsightly.

Red pepper: the most pungent of all spices, this is very hot and biting. Use it sparingly to lend excitement to canape spreads and salad dressings and (with lemon juice) as a 'spark up' marinade for grilled vegetables. Perfect for curry and barbecued vegetable sauces and for the hot vegetable ragouts of Africa and the Caribbean. As you will see from the recipes in this book, I am a hot red pepper enthusiast and like to use a pinch or two of cayenne pepper or, more often, crushed dried chillies, as a flavour enhancer for most dishes. It makes a great difference to the flavour of the finished dish.

Turmeric
Made from the dried and ground stem or root of a plant of the ginger family, turmeric is similar in flavour to ginger, but more discreet. Famous mainly for the rich yellow colour it gives to foods, turmeric is often used to colour and flavour mixed pickles and curry and mustard powders. Mistakenly, it is often used to replace saffron in Indian, Moroccan, Spanish and Italian cooking. Anyone who has ever tasted a *risotto milanese* or a Spanish paella made with turmeric instead of saffron will know the difference. The Moroccans and Spaniards make a colouring mix for 'saffron' dishes which combines turmeric, paprika, cayenne pepper and just a hint of powdered saffron to make a less expensive (but, I am afraid, less interesting) flavouring blend.

Soups

Cold Yogurt Soup

SERVES 8

2 medium-sized cucumbers
salt
1 garlic clove, cut in half
1 tablespoon red wine vinegar

1 teaspoon dill seeds
600ml/1 pint natural yogurt
olive oil
1 tablespoon chopped mint

1   Peel the cucumbers, cut them lengthways into quarters and cut each quarter into slices 0.25cm/⅛ inch thick. Place the slices in a bowl and sprinkle with a little salt.

2   Rub another bowl with the cut garlic clove. Discard the garlic and swirl the red wine vinegar around the bowl to collect the flavour. Add the dill seeds and natural yogurt and stir until the mixture is the consistency of a thick soup, adding cold water, if necessary. Pour the mixture over the cucumber slices and stir again.

3   Transfer the soup to 8 individual soup bowls, and sprinkle each with a little olive oil and chopped mint.

Green Gazpacho with Melon & Grapes

SERVES 4

600ml/2 pints vegetable stock
150ml/¼ pint dry white wine
1 medium garlic clove, finely chopped
¼ cucumber, peeled, seeded and
  cut into dice
1 yellow courgette, cut into dice
2 sticks of celery, cut into thin slices
4 small radishes, cut into
  thin slices
24–36 Muscat grapes, cut in half
  (or white grapes, left whole)
¼ teaspoon salt

¼ teaspoon cracked black pepper
1 pinch crushed dried chillies

Garnish
1 slice of chilled green melon
  (2.5cm/1 inch thick), cut into
  2.5cm/1 inch cubes
4 spring onions (green parts only) cut
  into 0.5cm/¼ inch segments
12 small sprigs watercress
6 ice cubes

1 In a bowl, combine the first 11 ingredients. Chill in the refrigerator for a minimum of 2 hours.

2 When ready to serve, add the diced melon, sliced green onions, small sprigs of watercress and ice cubes.

Jellied Gazpacho

SERVES 4

6 large ripe tomatoes, peeled, seeded
   and coarsely diced
1 medium onion, finely chopped
1 garlic clove, finely chopped
1 medium green pepper, deseeded and
   thinly sliced
½ a cucumber, peeled and
   thinly sliced

dash of Tabasco sauce
salt and freshly ground pepper
4 tablespoons olive oil
2 tablespoons white wine vinegar
800ml/1 ½ pints jellied vegetable
   consommé, chilled
1 tablespoon finely chopped parsley
lemon wedges

1 Combine the coarsely diced tomatoes, finely chopped onion and garlic and thinly sliced green pepper and cucumber in a porcelain or earthenware (not metal) bowl. Season with Tabasco, salt and freshly ground pepper to taste. Pour over the olive oil and white wine vinegar and marinate in the refrigerator for 15–20 minutes.

2 Fold the chilled jellied vegetable consommé and the finely chopped parsley into the soup.

3 Transfer the soup to a soup tureen or 4 individual soup bowls, and serve with lemon wedges.

Mexican Pumpkin Soup

SERVES 4

2 tablespoons butter
225g/8oz onions, finely chopped
1 garlic clove, finely chopped
2 medium-sized tomatoes, peeled,
   seeded and chopped
450g/1lb pumpkin, seeded, peeled
   and cut into chunks

600ml/1 pint vegetable stock
salt and freshly ground pepper
150ml/¼ pint single cream
few drops of Tabasco or any
   hot pepper sauce

1 Heat the butter in a saucepan and sauté the finely chopped onions until soft, but not browned. Add the chopped garlic and tomatoes, pumpkin chunks and vegetable stock and simmer, covered, until the pumpkin is tender, about 30 minutes.

2 Cool the mixture slightly, then put it through a sieve or reduce it to a coarse purée in a blender or food processor.

3 Return the mixture to the pan and season with salt and freshly ground pepper to taste. Add the single cream and Tabasco or hot pepper sauce.

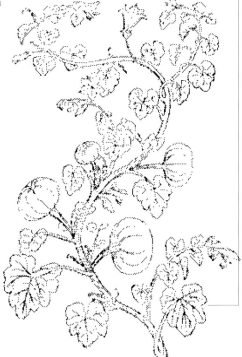

Cold Creamed Asparagus Soup

SERVES 4

450g/1lb frozen green asparagus
  spears
75g/3oz butter
600ml/1 pint hot vegetable stock
  (made with a cube)

salt and freshly ground pepper
pinch of cayenne pepper (optional)
150ml/¼ pint double cream

1 Reserve 8–12 asparagus tips for garnish and coarsely chop the remaining spears.

2 Melt the butter in a thick-bottomed saucepan and cook the coarsely chopped asparagus spears until limp. Transfer to the bowl of an electric blender or food processor and blend to a smooth purée.

3 Return the asparagus purée to the pan and add the hot vegetable stock. Season with salt and freshly ground pepper to taste, and cayenne pepper, if desired. Bring to the boil, lower the heat, and simmer for 5 minutes or until smooth and well blended.

4 Add the double cream and the reserved asparagus tips to the pan and continue cooking for a further 3 minutes or until the asparagus tips are just tender. Remove the pan from the heat, allow the soup to cool, then chill.

Quick Parsnip Bisque

SERVES 4

450g/1lb cooked parsnip, chopped
700ml/1 ¼ pints milk
1 vegetable stock cube
1 tablespoon flour
2 tablespoons butter
1 stick of celery, diced
1 thin slice onion

salt and freshly ground pepper
crushed dried chillies
1 carton crème fraîche

Garnish
garlic croûtons
1 tablespoon chopped parsley

1 Combine the first 7 ingredients in the container of an electric blender or food processor and blend until smooth. Season with salt, freshly ground pepper and crushed dried chillies to taste.

2 Pour the parsnip mixture into a thick-bottomed saucepan and bring just to the boil, stirring occasionally. Add crème fraîche and heat through.

3 Strain the bisque into a heated soup tureen or 4 individual soup bowls, and serve immediately, garnished with garlic croûtons and chopped parsley.

Creamed Mushroom Soup

SERVES 4

225g/8oz button mushrooms
50g/2oz butter
3 tablespoons flour
700ml/1¼ pints hot vegetable stock
juice of ½ a lemon

150ml/¼ pint double cream
2 tablespoons chopped parsley
salt and freshly ground pepper
freshly grated nutmeg

1 Wipe the mushrooms clean with a damp cloth and trim the stems. Thinly slice half and finely chop the remainder.

2 Melt the butter in a thick-bottomed saucepan, add the flour, and cook for 2–3 minutes, stirring constantly, until the flour is cooked through. Gradually add the hot vegetable stock and bring to the boil, stirring vigorously.

3 Add the thinly sliced mushrooms and the lemon juice to the pan and cook for 5 minutes. Pour the soup into the bowl of an electric blender or food processor and blend until smooth, then pass the mixture through a fine sieve.

4 Return the soup to a clean pan. Add the double cream, chopped parsley and finely chopped mushrooms, and season with salt, freshly ground pepper and freshly grated nutmeg to taste.

5 Transfer the soup to a heated soup tureen or 4 individual soup bowls.

Provençal Vegetable Soup with Pistou

SERVES 4 TO 6

salt
bouquet garni
1 large potato, peeled and diced
1 large onion, peeled and diced
1 stick of celery, scrubbed and
   finely sliced
2 carrots, scraped and sliced
225g/8oz French beans
225g/8oz runner beans
2 courgettes, topped and tailed,
   but unpeeled
100g/4oz pasta shells or macaroni

Pistou Sauce
3–4 large garlic cloves, peeled
4-6 tablespoons chopped sweet basil leaves
salt and freshly ground pepper
50g/2oz freshly grated Parmesan cheese
2 medium tomatoes, skinned, seeded
   and coarsely chopped
4 tablespoons olive oil

1 Bring 1.5 litres/3 pints water to the boil with 1 teaspoon salt in a large flameproof casserole. Add bouquet garni, prepared potato, onion, celery and carrots. Bring back to the boil, then cover and simmer for about 10 minutes or until the vegetables are almost tender.

2 Top and tail the French beans, remove any fibrous strings and cut the beans in half. Slice the runner beans into 1cm/½ inch lengths. Slice the courgettes thickly. Add the beans, courgettes and pasta to the casserole and simmer, uncovered, for 10–15 minutes until tender.

3 To make the pistou sauce, pound the garlic and chopped basil, with salt and freshly ground pepper to taste, to a paste using a mortar and pestle. Gradually work in the freshly grated Parmesan, alternating with the coarsely chopped tomatoes, then slowly work in the olive oil, a few drops at a time to start with, to make a thick sauce.

4 Remove the bouquet garni from the soup and discard. Blend 4 tablespoons of the hot soup into the sauce, then stir the mixture into the soup. Correct the seasoning.

Pimento and Corn Chowder

SERVES 4

15g/½oz butter
1 tablespoon flour
700ml/1¼ pints hot vegetable stock
½ can sweetcorn, drained
12 baby sweetcorn, cut into
  1cm/½ inch segments and blanched

1 canned red pimento, cut into thin strips
1–2 tablespoons lemon juice
1–2 teaspoons soy sauce
freshly ground pepper
crushed dried chillies
chopped fresh coriander

1 Melt the butter in a thick-bottomed saucepan; add the flour, and cook for 2–3 minutes, stirring constantly, until the flour is cooked through. Gradually add the hot vegetable stock and cook, stirring vigorously, until smooth and well blended.

2 Add the canned sweetcorn and blanched baby sweetcorn segments to the pan and season with lemon juice, soy sauce, freshly ground pepper and crushed dried chillies to taste. Bring to the boil and cook for 5–10 minutes, or until the baby sweetcorn are tender.

3 Add the red pimento strips and transfer the chowder to a heated soup tureen or 4 individual heated soup bowls. Garnish with a little chopped coriander.

Simple Starters

Black Olive Caviar

SERVES 4

185ml/7 fl oz jar black olives in brine
2 tablespoons chopped parsley
2 spring onions, thinly sliced
dash of soy sauce
1 teaspoon wine vinegar
3 tablespoons olive oil

freshly ground pepper
lettuce leaves
1 stick of celery, finely chopped
lemon twists
1 hard-boiled egg, sliced
crisp toast fingers and chilled butter

1 Wash the brine from the black olives, stone them and chop finely. Combine the chopped olives and parsley and the thinly sliced spring onions in a small bowl. Mix well.

2 Blend the soy sauce and wine vinegar in a small bowl. Add the olive oil and freshly ground pepper to taste, and stir until the sauce is smooth. Add this dressing to the chopped vegetable mixture. Toss until well mixed, then chill.

3 Just before serving, arrange some lettuce leaves around a small light–coloured hors d'œuvre dish. Stir the finely sliced celery into the olive mixture. Arrange the 'caviar' in the dish; garnish with lemon twists and sliced hard-boiled egg. Serve with crisp toast fingers and chilled butter.

Eggs in Aspic

SERVES 6

800ml/1 ½ pints Aspic (see below)
3 tablespoons Madeira
6 thin slices of cooked carrot
sprigs of tarragon or parsley
6 medium eggs

6 thin slices of cooked celeriac
6 small lettuce leaves
6 sprigs of watercress or parsley
12 black olives
tomato wedges

1 Warm the aspic until it liquefies, then stir in the Madeira. Pour a thin layer over the base of 6 individual ramekins, large enough to hold an egg. Refrigerate for 20 minutes or until set.

2 Cut the carrot slices into flower shapes and arrange them on top of the aspic. Surround them with small sprigs of tarragon or parsley to make 'leaves'. Spoon a 0.5cm/¼ inch layer of liquid aspic over them and chill again until set.

3 Poach the eggs lightly for 3 minutes. Allow them to cool and trim the edges neatly. Put one in each ramekin and fill to the brim with liquid aspic. Chill again until set.

4 Cut the celeriac slices to the diameter of the ramekins and fit them into each ramekin over the top of the solid aspic. Melt the remaining aspic and spoon a little over the ham. Chill until ready to serve.

5 To unmould, plunge each ramekin into hot water for 1–2 seconds and invert each one over an individual salad plate. Hold the plate and the ramekin together and shake gently until you feel the aspic loosen and settle onto the plate. If you are not serving them immediately, return the aspics to the refrigerator.

6 Just before serving, garnish each plate with a lettuce leaf, a sprig of watercress or parsley, 2 black olives and a tomato wedge or two.

To save time, you can make aspic from powdered gelatine and good-quality canned consommé (or use vegetarian aspic). Mix according to the instructions on the gelatine packet, You can also serve a smaller number of eggs in aspic on a single large serving plate. To do this, invert each ramekin on to a small damp plate and slide the aspics on to a larger damp serving plate.

Frozen Tomato Vodka

SERVES 6

300ml/10fl oz tomato juice
90ml/3fl oz Vodka
juice of 2 lemons
4–6 drops of Worcestershire sauce
6 ice cubes, crushed
½ green pepper, finely diced

4 celery leaves, chopped
2 slices of red onion, diced
¼ unpeeled cucumber, diced
celery salt and freshly ground pepper
6 cucumber sticks, 10cm/4 inches long
6 sprigs of mint or watercress
6 thin lemon slices (optional)

1 Place the tomato juice, vodka, lemon juice, Worcestershire sauce to taste, and crushed ice in an electric blender and blend at high speed for 1 minute or until the ice has completely disintegrated. Add the finely diced green pepper, chopped celery leaves and diced red onion and cucumber and season with celery salt and freshly ground pepper to taste.

2 Pour the mixture into freezer trays and freeze until the mixture begins to harden around the sides of the trays, about 1–2 hours. Beat the mixture with a whisk or fork and return to the freezer until firmly frozen, a minimum of 2–3 hours.

3 About 30 minutes before serving, transfer the frozen mixture to the refrigerator to soften.

4 Just before serving, spoon the tomato mixture into goblets, topping each serving with a cucumber stick or a thin lemon slice and a sprig of mint or watercress.

Tomato Cups with Green Dressing

SERVES 4–6

4–6 large ripe tomatoes
salt and freshly ground black pepper

Dressing
6 tablespoons chopped watercress leaves
6 tablespoons chopped spring onions
   (green part)
2 tablespoons chopped chives
1 garlic glove, finely chopped
6 tablespoons fresh breadcrumbs
2–3 tablespoons wine vinegar

8–12 tablespoons extra-virgin olive oil
salt and freshly ground pepper
cayenne pepper (or crushed
   dried chillies)

Garnish
8–12 asparagus spears, cut into
   4cm/1 ½ inch segments and
   lightly cooked
8–12 sprigs of watercress
thinly sliced white part of 2 spring onions

1 Dip the tomatoes quickly into boiling water, then into iced water. Peel them, cut off the top third of each tomato and scoop out 2.5cm/1 inch of the tomato pulp from each tomato to form cups. Place the tomato cups, cut side up, on a serving platter. Season the interiors with salt and freshly ground pepper. Cut the top of each tomato into small dice. Chill the tomato cups and the diced tomato flesh.

2 In a small bowl, combine the chopped watercress, green part of spring onions, chives, garlic and breadcrumbs with the diced tomato flesh. Add the wine vinegar and olive oil, and season with salt, freshly ground black pepper and cayenne (or crushed dried chillies) to taste.

3 To serve, spoon the dressing into the tomato cups and garnish each with 2 cooked asparagus spears (set vertically into each cup), 2 watercress sprigs and a scattering of rings of sliced white part of spring onion.

Tomatoes Guacamole

SERVES 4

8 large tomatoes

salt

2 avocado pears

juice of 1 lemon

1 garlic clove, mashed

1–2 tablespoons onion juice

freshly ground pepper

Mexican chile powder

2 sticks of celery, finely chopped

½ medium green pepper, finely chopped

1–2 tablespoons finely chopped

coriander or parsley

1 Prepare the tomato cases by plunging them into boiling water for a minute, one by one, and removing their skins with a sharp knife. Slice the cap off each tomato and carefully scoop out all the pulp and seeds. Season the inside of each tomato cup with a little salt and turn upside down on a tray to drain. Cover the tomato caps loosely with foil and chill.

2 Peel the avocados and mash lightly with a wooden spoon. Add the lemon juice and mashed garlic and season with onion juice, salt, freshly ground pepper and Mexican chile powder to taste. Fold in the finely chopped celery and pepper and chill.

3 Just before serving, fill each tomato cup with the avocado mixture and sprinkle with finely chopped coriander or parsley.

Note: if Mexican chile powder is unavailable, season guacamole mixture with a pinch or two of crushed dried chillies.

Red Orange and Red Pepper Salad

SERVES 4

1 small head of radicchio leaves
2 red peppers
2 blood oranges
1 bunch of watercress

½ head of curly endive
well-flavoured vinaigrette dressing
(see p. 57)
2 slices of red onion, separated into rings

1 Divide the radicchio into separate leaves. Halve the red peppers lengthwise, remove the seeds, and cut the peppers into thin strips or half rounds. Peel the blood oranges (removing all pith), and cut into round slices crosswise.

2 Remove the stalks from the watercress and divide the curly endive (using the tender pale leaves only). Make a well-flavoured vinaigrette dressing.

3 In a large bowl, toss the salad leaves gently in the vinaigrette; arrange the leaves in a salad bowl. Add the orange slices, pepper strips (or half rounds) and red onion rings to the vinaigrette and mix well. Arrange on the salad leaves, reserving 2 or 3 orange slices and red onion rings to arrange decoratively on top of the salad.

Corn Salad with Beetroot and Avocado

SERVES 4

225g/8oz corn salad (mâche)
225g/8oz jar diced beetroot, drained
6 tablespoons olive oil

2 tablespoons lemon juice
salt and freshly ground pepper

1 Wash the corn salad (mâche) and remove the stalks and any damaged leaves. Dry carefully with absorbent paper.

2 Rinse the diced beetroot. Drain.

3 Combine the olive oil and lemon juice in a salad bowl and season with salt and freshly ground pepper, to taste. Add the corn salad and beetroot and toss until all the ingredients glisten.

Beetroot and Cauliflower Salad Bowl

SERVES 4

1 small cauliflower
salt
150ml/¹/4 pint olive oil
3 tablespoons red wine vinegar
pinch of dried rosemary
2 tablespoons chopped parsley

freshly ground pepper
450g/1lb cooked beetroot, diced
1 medium stick of celery chopped
1 tablespoon finely chopped
  spring onion

1 Remove the green leaves from the cauliflower, trim the stem and cut off any bruised spots. Break into florets.

2 Cook the florets in lightly salted boiling water for 4–5 minutes or until just tender. Drain and refresh under cold running water. Drain again, and chill.

3 Combine the olive oil, red wine vinegar, dried rosemary and chopped parsley and season with salt and freshly ground pepper to taste.

4 Combine the chilled florets, diced beetroot, chopped celery and finely chopped spring onion in a salad bowl. Pour over the dressing and toss until all the ingredients glisten.

Pears with Roquefort and Watercress Dressing

SERVES 4

75g/3oz watercress
100g/4oz Roquefort cheese
2 large egg yolks
150ml/5fl oz olive oil
2 tablespoons lemon juice
freshly ground pepper

2 large ripe pears
2 tablespoons chopped walnuts

Decoration
1 bunch of watercress

1 Trim the watercress, discarding any discoloured leaves. Wash thoroughly and dry carefully in a teatowel

2 In a blender, combine 50g/2oz Roquefort, the watercress and the egg yolks and blend slowly, adding olive oil gradually as for a mayonnaise. Add 2 teaspoons lemon juice and freshly ground pepper, to taste.

3 Peel the pears and place in a bowl containing acidulated water, made with 300ml/10fl oz water and remaining lemon juice, to prevent discoloration.

4 Cover the base of 4 individual serving plates with the Roquefort mixture.

5 Quarter each pear, remove the core, and slice thinly. Arrange overlapping slices of pear down the centre of each plate. Crumble the remaining Roquefort and sprinkle over the pear slices with the chopped walnuts.

6 Decorate each plate with a small bouquet of watercress leaves.

Crisp Moroccan Salad

SERVES 4–6

1 green pepper
1 red pepper
1 yellow pepper
1 medium red onion
4 tomatoes
2 small aubergines
4 small courgettes
olive oil

2 garlic cloves, finely chopped
1–2 teaspoons paprika
salt and freshly ground pepper
1 small hot red pepper, thinly sliced
lemon juice
lettuce leaves
2 tablespoons finely chopped parsley

1 Remove the core and seeds from the peppers. Cut the peppers, onion and tomatoes into 1cm/½ inch dice.

2 Cut the unpeeled aubergines and courgettes into 1cm/½ inch dice. In a large heatproof frying pan, sauté the diced aubergines and courgettes in 6 tablespoons olive oil with the garlic, paprika and salt and freshly ground pepper to taste, until the vegetables are slightly softened.

3 Add the diced green, red and yellow peppers and onion to the pan (and a little more oil, if necessary), then stir well and continue to cook over a low heat until the vegetables are tender and still crisp, and the liquids have evaporated from the pan. Add the tomatoes and the thinly sliced hot red pepper; toss once, then remove the pan from the heat. Allow to cool.

4 When ready to serve, sprinkle the salad with olive oil and lemon juice to taste. Correct the seasoning, mix well, and pile high on lettuce leaves arranged in a ring on a serving plate. Sprinkle with the finely chopped parsley and serve immediately.

Gazpacho Salad

SERVES 8

2 medium Spanish onions
1 large cucumber
8 large tomatoes
1 large green pepper
8–12 tablespoons fresh
  breadcrumbs

6 tablespoons olive oil
2–3 tablespoons wine vinegar
1 garlic clove, crushed
generous pinch of powdered
  mustard
salt and freshly ground pepper

1 Slice the onions thinly and soak them in iced water for 1 hour. Drain.

2 Slice the unpeeled cucumber thinly. Peel and slice the tomatoes. Seed and core the peppers and cut into thin rounds.

3 Layer the prepared onion, cucumber, tomatoes and pepper alternately with the breadcrumbs in a large glass serving bowl.

4 Make a well-seasoned dressing with the remaining ingredients and pour over the salad. Chill before serving.

French Hors d'Oeuvre Trio

EACH RECIPE SERVES 4

Tomato Salad

4–6 ripe tomatoes
salt and freshly ground pepper

Vinaigrette dressing
6–8 tablespoons extra-virgin olive oil
2–3 tablespoons wine vinegar
2–3 tablespoons finely chopped parsley
1–2 garlic cloves, finely chopped

1 Wipe the tomatoes clean and slice them across into even slices. Place them in an hors d'œuvre dish.

2 *To make vinaigrette dressing:* in a small bowl, mix the olive oil, wine vinegar, and salt and freshly ground pepper to taste. Pour this dressing over the salad.

3 Sprinkle the salad with the finely chopped parsley and garlic, to taste.

Bean Salad Vinaigrette

700g/1 ½lb fine French beans
salt
6–8 tablespoons extra-virgin olive oil
2–3 tablespoons wine vinegar

freshly ground pepper
finely chopped parsley
finely chopped garlic

1 Top and tail the French beans and cook them in boiling salted water until just tender.

2 Drain the beans and toss them while still warm in a well-flavoured vinaigrette dressing (olive oil and wine vinegar seasoned with salt, freshly ground pepper and finely chopped parsley and garlic to taste).

Celeriac Salad with Mustard and Lemon Cream

2 celeriac roots, about 225g/8oz each
salt
2 tablespoons lemon juice

Mustard and Lemon Cream Sauce
6–8 tablespoons double cream
2–3 tablespoons olive oil

2–3 tablespoons lemon juice
2–3 tablespoons finely chopped onion
dry mustard
salt and freshly ground pepper
crushed dried chillies

Garnish
1 lemon (rind only), cut into thin strips

1   Scrub the celeriac roots with a stiff brush under running water to remove dirt. Cook the celeriac in boiling salted water until just tender. Cool, peel and cut into thin slices. Then cut each slice into thin strips. Toss with lemon juice and reserve.

2   To make the sauce, combine the double cream, olive oil, lemon juice and finely chopped onion in a bowl. Season with dry mustard, salt, freshly ground pepper and crushed dried chillies to taste. Mix well.

3   Marinate the celeriac strips in the mustard cream dressing overnight in the refrigerator. Garnish with thin strips of lemon zest.

Green Rice Salad with Green Vegetables

SERVES 6

150g/6oz spinach leaves
8 cauliflower florets
225g/8oz French beans, cut into
   1cm/½ inch segments
salt
1 tablespoon olive oil

2 medium courgettes, thinly sliced
150ml/¼ pint French dressing
450g/1lb cooked rice
4 tablespoons cooked peas
2 tablespoons finely chopped parsley

1 Wash the spinach leaves several times in cold water. Drain. Remove any coarse stems and damaged or yellowed leaves.

2 Cook the cauliflower florets, French bean segments and spinach in separate thick-bottomed saucepans of boiling salted water for 3–5 minutes or until just tender. Drain and refresh under cold running water. Drain again.

3 Press the raw spinach leaves between your hands to get rid of excess moisture. Chop finely.

4 Heat the olive oil in a thick-bottomed frying-pan and toss the thinly sliced courgettes in the oil for 1–2 minutes or until just tender. Remove from the pan with a slotted spoon. Allow to cool.

5 Combine the spinach with the French dressing.

6 Place the cooked rice in a salad bowl, add the spinach and toss until each grain of rice glistens. Add the prepared vegetables, cooked peas and finely chopped parsley, and toss again until all the ingredients are coated with dressing.

French Courgette Salad

SERVES 4

8 courgettes, 10cm/4 inches long
salt
½ Spanish onion, finely chopped
1 garlic clove, finely chopped
French dressing
lettuce leaves
4 tomatoes, peeled, seeded and
finely diced

½ small green pepper, finely diced
½ small orange pepper, finely diced
¼ Spanish onion, finely diced
1 tablespoon capers, finely chopped
1-2 teaspoons each finely chopped parsley
and basil
freshly ground pepper

1 Simmer the courgettes in salted water for about 8 minutes. Cut them in half lengthways and carefully scoop out the seeds. Lay the halved courgettes, cut sides up, in a flat dish.

2 Combine the finely chopped onion and garlic and sprinkle over the courgettes. Sprinkle over half of the French dressing, cover with foil, and allow to marinate in refrigerator for at least 4 hours.

3 Remove the onion and garlic mixture and drain off marinade. Arrange the courgettes on lettuce leaves and fill the hollows with the remaining French dressing, to which you have added finely chopped tomatoes, peppers, onion, capers, parsley, basil and salt and freshly ground pepper to taste.

Coleslaw with Pineapple, Green Pepper and Raisins

SERVES 6

4 tablespoons lemon juice
1 teaspoon salt
6 tablespoons mayonnaise
450g/1lb white cabbage,
  finely shredded
4 slices canned pineapple, cut into
  small wedges

1 small green pepper, seeded
  and chopped
50g/2oz raisins, blanched
4 tablespoons chopped parsley
2 sticks of celery, chopped
2 tablespoons finely chopped onion

1   Combine the lemon juice, salt and mayonnaise

2   Combine the finely shredded cabbage, pineapple wedges, chopped green pepper, raisins, chopped parsley and celery and finely chopped onion in a salad bowl. Add mayonnaise and toss lightly until all the ingredients are evenly coated. Chill.

Cheese and Walnut Roulade with Leaves of Green

SERVES 6

100g/4oz Danish blue cheese	cayenne pepper
100g/4oz full fat cream cheese	25g/1oz chopped walnuts
50g/2oz softened butter	mixed green salad
1 teaspoon Cognac	rounds of toast or cheese biscuits

1 Blend the blue cheese and cream cheese thoroughly in a food processor, or simply, with a wooden spoon. Add the softened butter and blend again until smooth.

2 Flavour the cheese mixture with Cognac and cayenne pepper, to taste.

3 Place the cheese mixture on a sheet of greaseproof paper and roll up (in the paper) into a 15cm/6 inch long sausage shape, securing the ends by twisting the paper. Chill until firm.

4 Remove the paper and roll the sausage-shaped cheese in the chopped walnuts. Cut into 12 slices with a very sharp knife (wiping the knife between each cut), and serve with a mixed green salad and rounds of toast or cheese biscuits.

Asparagus, Rocket and French Bean Salad with Parmesan Curls

SERVES 4

225g/8oz fine asparagus, trimmed and
   cut into 4cm/1½ inch segments
150g/6oz fine French beans
100g/4oz rocket leaves
50g/2oz corn salad (mâche) leaves
sprigs of fresh chervil
shavings of fresh Parmesan (grana) cheese

Dressing
9–12 tablespoons extra-virgin olive oil
2–3 tablespoons balsamic vinegar
1 garlic clove, finely chopped
salt and freshly ground pepper
1 pinch crushed dried chillies

1   In a large saucepan, cook the asparagus tips and uppermost tender segments in boiling salted water until just tender. Drain.

2   In a separate pan, cook the French beans in boiling salted water until just tender. Drain.

3   Wash the rocket leaves, corn salad and chervil sprigs, removing any damaged or yellowed leaves. Shake dry.

4   To make the dressing, combine the oil, vinegar and garlic in a small bowl and add salt, pepper and crushed dried chillies to taste.

5   To prepare the salad, combine the rocket and corn salad in a large bowl pour over one–third of the dressing and toss lightly.

6   Divide the remaining dressing between 2 small bowls. Add the asparagus to one and toss gently. Add the French beans to the other and toss gently. Arrange the asparagus segments and beans decoratively on the salad leaves and garnish with shavings of fresh Parmesan.

French Cucumber Salad

SERVES 4 TO 6

1 large cucumber
salt and freshly ground pepper
2 tablespoons wine vinegar
1 tablespoon Dijon mustard

6 tablespoons olive oil
2 tablespoons finely chopped tarragon
1 tablespoon finely chopped chives
4–6 tablespoons double cream

1 Peel and slice the cucumber thinly (a mandolin cutter is best for this). Place the cucumber slices in a glass bowl and toss with salt and freshly ground pepper to taste.

2 To prepare the dressing, beat half the wine vinegar and Dijon mustard until well mixed, add half the olive oil and season with salt and freshly ground pepper to taste. Beat again until the ingredients form an emulsion. Pour over the cucumber slices, toss, and chill for at least 30 minutes. Drain the dressing from the cucumber.

3 Make a second dressing with the remaining wine vinegar, Dijon mustard and olive oil and the finely chopped tarragon and chives. Season as above and pour over the salad. Toss well.

4 Whisk the double cream until stiff, add salt to taste, and spoon over the salad.

Orange and Onion Salad with Black Olives

SERVES 4–5

4 large oranges
1 large red onion
2 Little Gem lettuces
1 bunch watercress

Dressing
6 tablespoons olive oil
1–2 tablespoons balsamic vinegar
orange juice, left over from the sliced
  oranges

1–2 garlic cloves, finely chopped
salt and freshly ground pepper
crushed dried chillies

Garnish
12–18 black olives
2 tablespoons chopped flat-leafed
  parsley

1 With a sharp knife, peel the oranges, carefully removing all the white pith. Over a bowl (to catch juices) cut the oranges crosswise into thin slices. Cover the bowl with clingfilm and chill until ready to use.

2 Wash the lettuces and watercress and remove any damaged leaves. Dry the leaves carefully and arrange them in a large glass salad bowl, or in smaller, individual bowls.

3 Mix all the ingredients for the dressing adding the reserved orange juice. Just before serving, pour the dressing over the salad. Garnish with black olives and finely chopped flat-leafed parsley and serve immediately.

French Cucumber Salad (see p.66)

Orange and Onion Salad with Black Olives (see p.67)

First Courses and Supper Dishes

Italian Baked Asparagus

SERVES 4

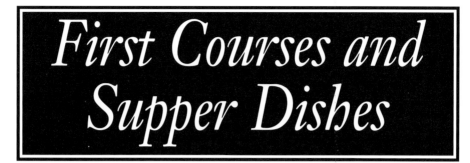

4 tablespoons butter
450g/1lb uncooked asparagus spears
4 tablespoons finely chopped onion
4 tablespoons finely chopped celery
2 tablespoons freshly grated
  Parmesan cheese
2 tablespoons fresh breadcrumbs
4 canned Italian peeled tomatoes, diced
salt and freshly ground pepper
pinch of dried oregano
pinch of dried thyme

1 Preheat the oven to 190°C/375°F/Gas 5

2 Melt the butter in the bottom of a rectangular baking dish.

3 Line the dish with asparagus spears. Sprinkle with finely chopped onion and celery, freshly grated Parmesan, breadcrumbs and diced tomatoes. Season with salt and freshly ground pepper, to taste, dried oregano and thyme, and bake in the preheated oven for about 45 minutes.

American Double Corn Croquettes

SERVES 6

3 tablespoons butter
5 tablespoons flour
400g/14oz can creamed corn
1 egg yolk
salt and freshly ground pepper

crushed dried chillies
185g/7oz can corn kernels, drained
1 egg, beaten
75g/3oz fresh white breadcrumbs
oil

1 In a medium-sized saucepan, melt the butter and add 3 tablespoons flour to form a pale roux. Cook for 1–2 minutes, stirring. Add the creamed corn, bring to the boil, reduce the heat to a simmer and cook for 5 minutes.

2 Remove the pan from the heat, stir in the egg yolk and season generously with salt, freshly ground pepper and crushed dried chillies to taste. Stir in the corn kernels.

3 Line a 16x16cm/7x7inch tin with clingfilm. Pour the corn mixture into the tin, spread evenly, and refrigerate until thoroughly chilled (about 1½ hours).

4 Place the remaining flour, beaten egg and breadcrumbs in separate flat containers. Divide the corn mixture into 12-18 portions. Shape into even-sized croquettes. Roll the croquettes in flour and beaten egg and coat with breadcrumbs. Chill for 30 minutes.

5 Heat the oil in a deep-fat frier to 350°F/180°C, or until a cube of stale bread dropped into the oil turns brown in 60 seconds. Deep-fry the croquettes for 1 minute or until golden brown. Drain on absorbent paper. Serve with red tomato salsa (page 219).

Pumpkin Terrine (see p.74)

Pumpkin Terrine

SERVES 6

900g/2lb pumpkin
2 large eggs
salt and freshly ground pepper
freshly grated nutmeg

300ml/10 fl oz double cream
1 tablespoon white wine vinegar
4–6 sorrel leaves, cut across the
  grain into very thin strips

1 Heat the oven to 180°C/350°F/Gas 4.

2 Remove the peel and seeds from the pumpkin and cut the flesh into large dice. Place the diced pumpkin in a flameproof casserole, add just enough water to cover, and bring to the boil. Cook until the pumpkin is just soft. Remove from the heat and drain off the liquid.

3 Purée the cooked pumpkin until smooth in a blender or food processor, adding the eggs, one at a time, as you blend. Season generously with salt, freshly ground pepper and freshly grated nutmeg.

4 Lightly butter the bottom and sides of a rectangular 600ml/1 pint terrine or pâté mould. Spoon the pumpkin purée into the mould and smooth the top with a spatula.

5 Place the terrine in a roasting tin, and pour enough hot water into the tin to come 2.5cm/1 inch up the sides of mould. Place the tin over a medium heat until the water comes to the boil, then transfer to the preheated oven. Reduce the heat to 170°C/325°F/Gas 3, and cook for 1 hour or until a skewer comes out clean when inserted in the centre. Cool to room temperature.

6 Bring the double cream gently to the boil with the white vinegar and simmer gently for 10–15 minutes or until the sauce has thickened. Season with salt and freshly ground pepper, to taste, cover with buttered greaseproof paper, and chill.

7 Just before serving, ease a knife around the sides of the terrine to loosen the edges and turn out on to a flat plate. Cut the terrine into 6 slices and place on individual serving plates. Pour a little sauce around each slice of terrine and sprinkle with sorrel strips.

Roasted Peppers with Garlic

SERVES 8–10

6 large peppers, a combination of
   yellow, red and green
6–8 tablespoons olive oil
2 tablespoons wine vinegar
salt and freshly ground pepper
pinch of dried thyme

¼ teaspoon ground fennel seeds or
   celery salt
100g/4oz green olives, stoned
1–2 tablespoons finely chopped garlic
2 tablespoons finely chopped parsley

1 Heat the grill to maximum for 20 minutes. Arrange the peppers in the grill pan, reduce the heat to moderate, and grill the peppers until their skins blacken and blister, turning them regularly so that they cook evenly. Do not increase the heat again – slow steady charring gives the peppers their delicious flavour.

2 When the peppers are thoroughly charred all over, place them under cold running water and rub off the skins with your fingers. Pat the peppers dry, cut them in half and discard the seeds and stems. Slice the peppers into thick strips.

3 In a small bowl, combine the olive oil and wine vinegar and season with salt and freshly ground pepper, to taste. Add the dried thyme and ground fennel seeds or celery salt and whisk vigorously with a fork until emulsified.

4 Arrange the pepper strips in a shallow dish. Pour over the dressing and toss lightly. Cover the dish with foil, place in the refrigerator, and leave to marinate for 8 hours or overnight.

5 Just before serving, arrange the peppers in a large serving dish. Garnish with the green olives and sprinkle with the finely chopped garlic and parsley.

Baked Peppers Stuffed with Ricotta and Parmesan Cheese

SERVES 4–5

25g/1oz butter
2 tablespoons olive oil
150–225g/6–8oz onion, chopped
1 garlic clove, chopped
150–225g/6–8oz easy-cook
   Italian rice
4–5 plump peppers
325ml/11 fl oz vegetable stock
2 hard-boiled eggs

4 tablespoons freshly grated
   Parmesan cheese
100g/4 oz Ricotta cheese, chopped
100g/4 oz walnuts, chopped
2 tablespoons chopped parsley
1 teaspoon dried oregano
salt and freshly ground pepper
100g/4oz mozzarella cheese, cut
   into 4 slices

1 Preheat the oven to 180°C/350°F/Gas 4.

2 Heat the butter and olive oil in a large saucepan over a medium heat and sauté the chopped onion and garlic until soft. Add the rice and continue cooking, stirring, for about 2 minutes.

3 Slice the lids from the peppers and seed them. Parboil the peppers for 10 minutes, then drain and set them aside upside down.

4 Chop the pepper lids and add to the rice. Add the vegetable stock, stir once, cover, and cook for 12 minutes, adding more stock if necessary.

5 Chop the hard-boiled eggs and add to the rice together with the freshly grated Parmesan, chopped Ricotta, walnuts, parsley and dried oregano. Season with salt and freshly ground pepper to taste.

6 Arrange the peppers in a buttered baking dish into which they fit snugly. Fill with the stuffing, top with the mozzarella slices, and bake in preheated oven for 30 minutes.

Do not try to economize by omitting the Parmesan, which is needed to flavour the rice, but you can use Cheddar instead of Mozzarella for the topping of this three-cheese dish.

Roasted Peppers with Tomatoes

SERVES 4–6

6 tablespoons olive oil
3 large green peppers
6 ripe tomatoes
2 garlic cloves, finely chopped
2 tablespoons finely chopped coriander leaves

¼–½ teaspoon powdered cumin
¼ teaspoon paprika
⅛ teasponn cayenne pepper
salt and freshly ground pepper
juice of ½ –1 lemon

1 In a large heatproof frying pan, heat the olive oil. Sauté the halved green peppers until soft and just beginning to change colour.

2 Cut the tomatoes in half and gently squeeze out the liquid and seeds. Place the tomatoes, cut sides up, in the pan and continue to cook, shaking the pan from time to time (and turning the peppers occasionally) until the tomatoes are cooked through. Transfer the tomatoes and peppers to a serving dish.

3 Pour off half the olive oil left in the frying pan, and return the pan to the heat. Add the finely chopped garlic and coriander and sauté for 1 minute over a high heat. Remove the pan from the heat and season the oil in the pan with the cumin, paprika and cayenne pepper, adding salt and freshly ground pepper to taste. Add the lemon juice and spoon this sauce over the tomatoes and green peppers. Serve warm or cold.

Trio of Vegetables à la Grècque

ALL RECIPES SERVE 4

Mushrooms à la Grècque

450g 1lb button mushrooms, thickly sliced
2 tablespoons chopped coriander or flat-leafed parsley

Bouillon
4 tablespoons tomato puree

4 tablespoons olive oil
6 tablespoons dry white wine
½ a Spanish onion, finely chopped
1 garlic clove, finely chopped
8 whole coriander seeds
¼ teaspoon saffron powder
salt and freshly ground pepper

1 For the bouillon, combine the tomato purée and 200ml/8 fl oz water in a saucepan with the olive oil, dry white wine, finely chopped onion and garlic, whole coriander seeds, saffron powder, and salt and freshly ground pepper to taste. Mix well, cover the pan, and bring to the boil. Simmer gently over the lowest possible heat for 20–30 minutes, stirring from time to time, adding a little water, if necessary.

2 Add the thickly sliced button mushrooms to the bouillon and simmer, uncovered, for 20 minutes. Transfer the mushrooms and reduced bouillon to a serving dish and leave to cool completely. Chill.

3 Just before serving, sprinkle with the chopped coriander or flat-leafed parsley.

Cauliflower Florets à la Grècque

1 large cauliflower, cut into florets
salt
2 tablespoons olive oil
1 tablespoon lemon juice
2 tablespoons finely chopped coriander or flat-leafed parsley

Bouillon
5 tablespoons tomato purée
5 tablespoons olive oil
5 tablespoons dry white wine
1 Spanish onion, finely chopped
12 coriander seeds, lightly crushed
salt and freshly ground pepper
pinch each of cayenne pepper and ground ginger

1 Blanch the cauliflower florets by cooking them in boiling salted water for 5 minutes.

2 For the bouillon, place the first 5 ingredients in a saucepan with 450ml/15 fl oz water. Season with salt and freshly ground pepper to taste, and add the cayenne pepper and ground ginger. Bring the mixture to the boil, skim the surface, then reduce the heat and simmer for 20 minutes.

3 Add the blanched cauliflower to the pan and simmer for a further 20–30 minutes until the cauliflower is tender. Transfer the cauliflower and reduced bouillon to a serving dish and leave to cool completely. Chill.

4 Just before serving, stir in the olive oil and lemon juice and sprinkle with the finely chopped coriander or flat-leafed parsley.

Button Onions à la Grècque

450g/1 lb small button onions
coarsely chopped parsley

Bouillon
50g/2 oz raisins, soaked overnight
* in water*
125–170ml/4–6 fl oz dry white wine

50g/2oz sugar
2 tablespoons tomato purée
4 tablespoons olive oil
½ vegetable stock cube, crumbled
2 tablespoons wine vinegar
salt and freshly ground pepper
cayenne pepper

1 To peel the button onions without making your eyes water, bring a large saucepan of water to the boil and drop in half the onions. Remove the pan from the heat. Lift out the onions one by one and slip off the skins. Repeat with remaining onions. Place the peeled onions in a saucepan with 300ml/½ pint water.

2 For the bouillon, drain the plumped-up raisins and add to the pan with the dry white wine, sugar, tomato purée, olive oil, crumbled vegetable stock cube and wine vinegar. Season with salt, freshly ground pepper and cayenne pepper to taste.

3 Bring the mixture to the boil, then reduce the heat and simmer for 30–40 minutes until the onions are tender but still quite firm. Add a little water to the bouillon during cooking, if necessary.

4 Transfer the onions and bouillon to a serving dish and leave to cool. Chill.

5 Just before serving, garnish with coarsely chopped parsley.

Deep-fried Camembert with Crisp Apple Slices

SERVES 4–6

1 cos lettuce	crushed dried chillies
1 head of chicory	2 Granny Smith apples
12 sprigs of watercress	juice of 1 lemon
olive oil	4 oz Camembert cheese, without rind
1–2 tablespoons balsamic vinegar	1–2 large eggs, beaten
salt and freshly ground pepper	50–75g/2–3 oz fresh breadcrumbs

1   Thoroughly wash and dry the lettuce, chicory and watercress. Wrap in tea-towels and store in the refrigerator to crisp for a minimum of 1 hour.

2   Combine 8 tablespoons olive oil with the balsamic vinegar and season with salt, freshly ground pepper and crushed dried chillies to taste. Mix well.

3   Toss the lettuce, chicory and watercress individually in vinaigrette. Arrange the lettuce around the edge of an oblong serving dish. Arrange the chicory leaves in the centre and scatter with sprigs of watercress.

4   Core the apples, cut into thin wedges and soak in lemon juice.

5   Heat sufficient olive oil for deep-frying to 180°C/350°F on a deep-fat thermometer, or until a cube of stale bread dropped into the oil turns brown in 60 seconds.

6   Use the cheese straight from the refrigerator, as it is easier to handle. Cut it into even wedges. Coat the cheese first in beaten egg and then in breadcrumbs and deep-fry for 2 minutes or until golden brown. Be careful not to overcook and allow the cheese to become too hot. Drain on absorbent paper.

7   To serve, arrange the cheese and apple wedges with the salad.

French Aubergine Pâté

SERVES 4

1 large aubergine, diced
4 tablespoons olive oil
salt and freshly ground pepper
crushed dried chillies
2 tablespoons mayonnaise
2 tablespoons double cream
lemon juice
toast or thin slices of rye or
  pumpernickel bread
sieved hard-boiled egg yolks or finely
  chopped parsley

1 Sauté the diced aubergine in the olive oil, stirring constantly, until golden brown on all sides. Season with salt and freshly ground pepper and crushed dried chillies, to taste.

2 Combine the aubergine, mayonnaise and double cream in a blender. Season with lemon juice to taste, and blend until smooth. Correct the seasoning, adding a little more salt, freshly ground pepper and crushed dried chillies if desired.

3 Serve the pâté on toast or thin slices of rye or pumpernickel bread, garnished with sieved hard-boiled egg yolks or finely chopped parsley.

Saffron Mushrooms in a Brioche Shell

SERVES 6

6 small brioches
melted butter
4 tablespoons freshly grated
   Parmesan cheese

Saffron Mushroom filling
juice of 1 lemon
1 garlic clove, finely chopped
1 medium onion, finely chopped
1 bay leaf
8 coriander seeds
8 black peppercorns

¼-½ teaspoons saffron
1 strip of lemon peel
¼ crumbled vegetable stock cube
8 tablespoons olive oil
300ml/ ½ pint dry white wine
700g/1 ½ lb small button mushrooms

To serve
1–2 tablespoons olive oil
2 tablespoons finely chopped coriander
salt
lemon juice

1 Preheat the oven to 150°C/300°F/Gas 2. In a small saucepan, combine the lemon juice, finely chopped onion and garlic, bay leaf, coriander seeds, peppercorns, saffron, lemon peel, crumbled vegetable stock cube, olive oil and dry white wine. Bring the mixture to the boil, skim the surface, then reduce the heat and simmer for 20 minutes.

2 Meanwhile, cut a slice from the top of each brioche and carefully scoop out two-thirds of the insides to form an edible container for the mushrooms. Brush the tops and cases with melted butter, sprinkle with freshly grated Parmesan, and place in the oven for 5 minutes. Keep warm.

3 Wash and trim the mushrooms. Add to saffron sauce and cook until just tender. Drain the mushrooms over a bowl to catch the saffron pan juices. Keep warm. Boil the reserved pan juices rapidly until thickened. Stir in the extra olive oil, chopped coriander and salt and lemon juice, to taste.

4 To serve, place 1 hot brioche case on each salad or dessert plate. Sprinkle 2 tablespoons of the reduced saffron sauce into each case and divide the mushrooms between them (spooning any extra mushrooms on to the plates). Add the brioche tops and serve immediately.

Papaya and Three-Bean Salad

SERVES 4-6

2-3 ripe papayas
1 x 400g/14oz can chick peas
1 x 400g/14oz can red kidney beans
1 x 400g/14oz can white beans

Dressing
8–12 tablespoons olive oil
2–3 tablespoons balsamic vinegar
½ a vegetable stock cube, crumbled

1 red onion, finely chopped
2 garlic cloves finely chopped
2 tablespoons finely chopped flat-
    leafed parsley
2 tablespoons finely chopped
    coriander leaves
salt and freshly ground pepper
crushed dried chillies

1 With a sharp knife, carefully peel the papayas. Cut each papaya in half and, with a teaspoon, remove the seeds. Lay the papaya halves, flat side down, on a working surface, and carefully slice off top rounded sides, leaving 1 fat slice from each papaya half (approximately 1–2cm/¼–½ inch thick).

2 Open the 3 cans (chick peas, red kidney beans and white beans), pour the contents of each can into a sieve and rinse well under cold running water, then drain.

3 In a large bowl, combine the drained chick peas and beans. Add the olive oil, balsamic vinegar, crumbled vegetable stock cube, finely chopped onion, garlic, flat-leafed parsley and coriander leaves and mix well. Season with salt, freshly ground pepper and crushed dried chillies to taste.

4 *To serve:* arrange papaya slices in a ring on a large serving dish. Spoon over the chick pea and bean salad (reserving any extra chick peas and beans to garnish a green salad at another meal). Serve immediately.

Couscous Salad with Spicy Vinaigrette

SERVES 6

225g/8oz couscous
600ml/1 pint vegetable stock, made with
  a cube
4 tablespoons olive oil
4 sun-dried tomatoes, cut into strips
½ teaspoon powdered cumin
¼ teaspoon paprika
¼ teaspoon cayenne pepper
lettuce leaves

Vinaigrette Dressing
6 tablespoons olive oil
2 tablespoons wine vinegar
4 tablespoons finely chopped red onion
1 garlic clove, finely chopped
1 pinch each powdered cumin, paprika and
  cayenne pepper
salt and freshly ground pepper

Garnish
½ can chick peas, rinsed under
  running water
6 spring onions, cut into 0.5cm/¼ inch
  segments
6 tablespoons chopped mint leaves

1 In a saucepan, combine the couscous, vegetable stock and olive oil and bring to the boil, stirring constantly. Add the sun-dried tomatoes, powdered cumin, paprika and cayenne pepper and mix well. Cover the saucepan and remove from the heat. Let stand for 5 minutes. Drain off any excess liquid and fluff the couscous with a fork.

2 Combine the olive oil, wine vinegar, chopped red onion and garlic, and salt and freshly ground pepper to taste, in a small bowl. Pour over the couscous salad and mix well.

3 To serve, transfer the couscous salad to a lettuce-lined salad bowl. Garnish with the drained chick peas, spring onion segments and chopped mint. Serve immediately.

Artichoke Heart and Two-Bean Salad

SERVES 4

8 cooked (or canned) artichoke hearts
225g/8oz fine French beans
400g/14 oz can flageolet beans
8 tiny sprigs curly endive
8 cherry tomatoes

Vinaigrette Dressing
8 tablespoons extra-virgin olive oil
2 tablespoons balsamic or red
   wine vinegar

1 garlic clove, finely chopped
salt and freshly ground pepper
pinch of crushed dried chillies
lemon juice

Garnish
chopped coriander
4 tiny springs of basil

1   Drain cooked (or canned) artichoke hearts. Cut 4 of them into quarters.

2   Top and tail the French beans and cook them in boiling salted water until just tender. Drain and cut into 3cm/1¼inch lengths.

3   Drain the flageolet beans under running water. Wash the curly endive and pat dry. Cut the cherry tomatoes in half.

4   To make the vinaigrette dessing, combine the olive oil and vinegar in a small bowl, and add the garlic, salt, pepper, crushed dried chillies and lemon juice to taste. Mix well.

5   To assemble the salads, arrange each whole cooked artichoke heart on a plate and spoon a little of the vinaigrette dressing over each one. Place the French bean segments in a small bowl; add half the remaining vinaigrette dressing and toss well. Toss the drained flageolet beans in the remaining dressing. Scatter the bean segments and flageolets over the artichoke heart in the centre of each plate. Arrange some sprigs of curly endive and halved cherry tomatoes, on each plate, and place 4 artichoke quarters around each salad. Garnish with the coriander and basil.

Moroccan Trio

EACH RECIPE SERVES 4

Schlada - Grilled Pepper & Tomato Salad

2-3 large green peppers
3-4 large beefsteak tomatoes

1 medium-sized red onion, finely chopped
salt, lemon juice

1 To prepare vegetables for salad: char green peppers under a hot grill until skins blister and turn black. Place charred peppers in a plastic bag and leave to sweat until cool enough to handle, then under running cold water, peel off skins. Pat peppers dry and dice evenly. Drain and chill diced peppers while you prepare tomatoes.

2 Place tomatoes (one by one) on the prongs of a kitchen fork and dip for 1 minute in boiling water and then 1 minute in iced water. Peel tomatoes, then press them gently to expel seeds and excess juices. Dice tomatoes, drain and chill.

3 When ready to serve, combine drained, chilled vegetables in a bowl; stir in chopped red onion and season with lemon juice and salt, to taste. Mix well.

Diced Lemon, Red Onion & Parsley Salad

4 large ripe lemons (thin-skinned)
1 large red onion

1 ½ bunches flat-leafed parsley
salt, lemon juice

1 Peel lemons, cutting away all white pith, then cut lemon flesh into small dice. Peel red onion and cut into slices. Cut each slice into small dice. Combine diced lemon and red onion in a bowl.

2 Coarsely chop flat-leafed parsley and add to other ingredients. Season with salt, moisten with a little lemon juice and mix well. Chill until ready to serve.

Chopped Aubergine Salad

2 aubergines (450g/1lb each)
2-3 cloves garlic
1-2 teaspoons paprika
¼-½ teaspoon cayenne pepper
½-1 teaspoon powdered cumin

Dressing
2-4 tablespoons olive oil
2-4 tablespoons lemon juice
salt, freshly ground pepper
crushed dried chillies

1 *To prepare aubergines:* cut crosswise into 1.25cm/½ inch slices. Heat 2 tablespoons olive oil in a thick-bottomed frying pan and fry the aubergine slices a few at a time, over a high heat until they are golden brown on both sides, adding a little more oil from time to time if necessary. Drain off excess oil.

2 Chop aubergine slices coarsely then mix with garlic and spices. Return to frying pan and continue to fry until all excess liquid evaporates.

3 Transfer aubergines to a salad bowl. Sprinkle with olive oil and lemon juice, and add salt, freshly ground black pepper and crushed dried chillies to taste. Garnish with chopped parsley, half lemon slices and black olives.

Stuffed Spanish Onions

SERVES 4

4 baked or boiled Spanish onions	*1 egg yolk*
2 slices of white bread	*salt and freshly ground pepper*
100g/4oz cooked spinach, chopped	*6 tablespoons fresh breadcrumbs*
150g/6oz blanched courgette, chopped	*4 tablespoons melted butter*
4 tablespoons chopped parsley	*1 tablespoon olive oil*

1 Preheat the oven to 190°C/375°F/Gas 5. Cut the onions in half horizontally. Remove the layers from the centre of each half, leaving a shell about 0.5cm/¼ inch thick. Coarsely chop the removed onion layers.

2 Soak the bread slices in water. Squeeze them until they are almost dry and shred them coarsely. Combine the coarsely chopped onion with the bread, chopped courgette and parsley. Moisten the mixture with the egg yolk and season with salt and freshly ground pepper to taste.

3 Mound the mixture into the onion shells, top with the breadcrumbs, and spoon over the melted butter and olive oil. Bake in the preheated oven for 15–20 minutes or until the breadcrumbs are golden brown.

Hot Curried Eggs with Mango Chutney

SERVES 4–6

6 hard-boiled eggs
2 tablespoons butter
6 tablespoons finely chopped onion
1 ½ tablespoons flour
1-2 teaspoons curry paste
300ml/ ½ pint hot vegetable stock
4 tablespoons double cream
1–2 teaspoons mango chutney

salt and freshly ground pepper
lemon juice

To serve
Plain boiled rice
Mango chutney

1 Cool the hard-boiled eggs under cold running water, then carefully peel off the shells and cut the eggs in half lengthwise.

2 In a heavy-bottomed saucepan, melt the butter and sauté the finely chopped onion, stirring constantly, for 4–5 minutes, or until soft and golden. Stir in the flour and curry paste and cook for a further 2–3 minutes, stirring constantly.

3 Add the hot vegetable stock, a little at a time, stirring vigorously with a whisk to prevent lumps forming. Then bring the mixture to the boil, stirring, and simmer for 30 minutes, or until the sauce is thick and smooth and no longer tastes raw.

4 Remove the pan from the heat, beat in the cream and chutney, and season to taste with salt, freshly ground pepper and a few drops of lemon juice to bring out the flavours.

5 Fold in the halved hard-boiled eggs and return the pan to a low heat for 3–4 minutes to heat them through. Serve immediately over plain boiled rice, and accompany with a bowl of mango chutney.

Thai Aubergine Sates (see p.94)

Crisp Vegetable and Tofu Brochettes (see p.95)

Thai Aubergine Sates

SERVES 4 AS A STARTER

550g/1 ¼lb aubergine (or 4 small
 Greek aubergines)
1 tablespoon curry powder
¼ teaspoon ground coriander
¼ teaspoon turmeric
pinch of cayenne pepper
freshly ground salt
3 tablespoons peanut oil

Thai Peanut Sauce
125ml/4 fl oz coconut cream
100g/4oz salted peanuts
½ teaspoon turmeric
½ teaspoon curry powder
¼ teaspoon cayenne pepper
2 tablespoons sugar
1 teaspoon lemon juice
salt

1 Cut the aubergine into thin long slices then cut each slice into 2.5x5cm/1x2 inch rectangles. Place the aubergine strips in a bowl and add the curry powder, ground coriander, turmeric, cayenne pepper and salt to taste.

2 Wet your hands and gently knead the spices into the aubergine strips, adding 1 teaspoon each of peanut oil and water to help work in the spice mixture. Knead again. Cover the bowl and leave for 2 hours.

3 To make the Thai peanut sauce, grind the peanuts coarsely (I use a clean electric coffee grinder). Add the turmeric, curry powder and cayenne pepper to the coconut cream and cook over a medium heat, stirring until the sauce comes to the boil. Reduce heat to low and add the peanuts. Continue to cook, stirring constantly, for 2 minutes. Add the lemon juice and salt to taste. Remove sauce from the heat and cool.

4 Thread 8 thin metal or bamboo skewers with 4 pieces of aubergine each. The skewers enter the aubergine 2 to 3 times like a needle threading through cloth.

5 Heat the grill to high. Brush the aubergine sates with the remaining peanut oil and grill 4 inches from the heat, turning frequently, until the sates are cooked through (4–6 minutes on each side).

6 Serve 2 skewers per person, and garnish each plate with Thai peanut sauce.

Crisp Vegetable and Tofu Brochettes

SERVES 4

2 medium carrots
2 small Greek aubergines
1 square of fresh tofu
4 small patty pan squash (or 1
   yellow courgette)
1 medium courgette
8 bamboo skewers, soaked in water for
   30 minutes
Red Tomato Salsa (see p. 219)

Greek yogurt
thin slices of spring onion

Marinade
6–8 tablespoons olive oil
1–2 tablespoons soy sauce
1 garlic clove, finely chopped
4 tablespoons red onion, finely chopped
pinch crushed dried chillies

1 Scrape carrots and cut them into 4 x 2.5cm/1 inch rounds. Cut unpeeled aubergines (the slender violet-coloured Greek ones) into 16 x 2.5cm/1 inch rounds. (If only the larger aubergines are available, cut 1 larger aubergine into 16 x 2.5cm/1 inch cubes. Cut the tofu into 16 x 2.5cm/1 inch cubes. Cut 4 small yellow patty pan squash into quarters. If not available, cut 1 small yellow courgette into 2.5cm/1inch rounds.

2 To make the marinade, combine the olive oil, soy sauce, finely chopped garlic and red onion and crushed dried chillies to taste in a shallow soup bowl. Add the prepared vegetables and tofu to the bowl and toss so that the vegetables and tofu are impregnated with sauce. Allow the vegetables and tofu to marinate in a cool place in this mixture for at least 30 minutes, tossing the vegetables and tofu in the marinade at least once during this time to keep them well coated.

3 When ready to cook, preheat the grill for 20 minutes. In the meantime, thread 1 piece each of carrot, aubergine, tofu and yellow squash (or yellow courgette) and courgette on to each skewer.

4 Grill for 6–8 minutes, or until the vegetables are crisp-tender, turning the skewers from time to time so that they cook evenly.

5 Serve with Red Tomato Salsa and Greek yogurt garnished with thin slices of spring onion.

Vegetable Salad Stroganoff

SERVES 8

225g/8oz potatoes, peeled
150g/6oz carrots, scraped
100g/4oz swede or turnip, peeled
50g/2 oz frozen peas
salt
50g/2oz diced celery
50g/2oz diced dill pickles
6 tablespoons spring onions tops, cut
   into 0.5cm/¼ inch slices

5 tablespoons mayonnaise
5 tablespoons crème fraîche
1 teaspoon French mustard
lemon juice
freshly ground pepper
16 lettuce leaves
16 slices hard-boiled egg
4 tablespoons finely chopped parsley

1 Cut the potatoes, carrots and swede or turnip into 0.5cm/¼ inch dice. Cook the diced vegetables and the peas separately in boiling, lightly salted water until just tender. Drain, refresh under cold running water and leave to cool.

2 Place the cooked vegetables in a large mixing bowl. Add the diced celery and dill pickles and the spring onion slices. Using a large serving fork, mix the ingredients together thoroughly, but gently, to avoid breaking the softer vegetables.

3 In a small bowl, combine the mayonnaise and *crème fraîche* with the French mustard and lemon juice and freshly ground pepper to taste, then fold into the vegetables. Place 2 lettuce leaves on each individual plate, spoon the salad onto the centre of the leaves and garnish with the slices of hard-boiled egg and the finely chopped parsley.

Roasted Pepper Mousse in Lemon Shells

SERVES 4

2-3 red peppers
4 large lemons
150g/6oz Philadelphia cream cheese
6 tablespoons crème fraîche
½ teaspoon Dijon mustard
1 teaspoon finely chopped onion
¼ teaspoon salt

½ teaspoon paprika
freshly ground pepper
cayenne pepper
1 egg white
4 sprigs of fresh thyme, bay leaves or
   chopped parsley

1 Heat the grill to maximum heat for 20 minutes. Arrange the peppers in the grill pan, reduce the heat to moderate, and grill the peppers until their skins blacken and blister, turning them regularly so that they cook evenly. Do not increase the heat again – slow steady charring gives the peppers their distinctive flavour.

2 When the peppers are thoroughly charred all over, place them under cold running water and rub off the skins with your fingers. Pat the peppers dry, cut them in half and discard the seeds and stems. Slice the peppers into thick strips.

3 Cut the tops off the lemons and reserve. Dig out the pulp with a grapefruit knife and/or a small spoon. Remove the pips and reserve the pulp and juice. Trim the bottoms of the lemons so they stand upright. If the lemons are thick-skinned, cut any excess pith from the insides with the grapefruit knife.

4 Mash the pepper strips to a smooth paste with the cream cheese, crème fraîche and Dijon mustard and the finely chopped onion. Season with salt, paprika and freshly ground pepper and cayenne pepper to taste. Strain the juice and pulp of 1 lemon into a small bowl. Add just enough strained juice and pulp to the pepper mousse to flavour to your taste.

5 Beat the egg white stiffly and fold into the mixture. Stuff the lemons, piling mousse up slightly into each lemon. Top with the lemon caps and chill until ready to serve. Before serving, tuck a sprig of thyme, a bay leaf or some chopped parsley into each lemon.

Savoury Bread and Butter Pudding

SERVES 4

75g/3oz butter, softened
½ onion, finely chopped
½ vegetable stock cube, crumbled
4 sun-dried tomatoes, diced
12 black olives, pitted and chopped
5 thin slices white bread, crusts
  removed

50g/2oz Emmenthal cheese
2 eggs + egg yolk
300ml/½ pint milk
salt and freshly ground pepper
pinch crushed dried chillies

1 In a small saucepan, melt 2 tablespoons butter. Stir in the chopped onion and the crumbled vegetable stock cube and cook over a medium heat, stirring constantly, for 5 minutes, or until the onion is transparent. Add the chopped sun-dried tomato and black olives to the mixture and reserve.

2 Butter an ovenproof dish. Butter the bread slices with the remaining butter. Cut each slice into 2 triangles and arrange half, butter side up, in the dish. Sprinkle over half the cheese and half the onion, tomato and olive mixture.

3 Arrange the remaining bread slices on top, butter side down. Sprinkle over the remaining cheese and onion, tomato and olive mixture.

4 In a bowl, beat the eggs, egg yolk and milk together. Season with salt, freshly ground pepper and dried chillies to taste, and slowly pour the egg mixture over the bread and butter. Cover the dish and set aside for 30 minutes to let the bread soak and become light-textured.

5 In the meantime, pre-heat the oven to 180°C/350°F/Gas 4. Uncover the pudding and bake just above the centre of the oven for 40–45 minutes, or until the top has browned and the custard has set. Serve immediately.

Potato & Celery Cake

SERVES 4

700g/1½ lb potatoes, peeled
salt
150ml/¼ pint double cream
3 tablespoons chopped onion
3 sticks of celery, chopped
115g/4¼ oz butter

4–6 tablespoons freshly grated Gruyère
freshly ground pepper
cayenne pepper
freshly grated nutmeg

Red Tomato Salsa (page 219)

1 Cook the potatoes in boiling salted water until soft; drain and mash with the double cream until smooth. In a frying pan, sauté the chopped onion and celery in 50g/2oz butter for about 4 minutes or until the celery and onion are translucent; then spoon the celery and onion mixture (with the pan juices) into the creamed potatoes. Season with freshly grated Gruyère, salt and freshly ground pepper, cayenne pepper and freshly grated nutmeg to taste. Mix well.

2 Heat 50g/2oz butter in a clean frying pan and add the potato and celery mixture. With a spatula, spread the mixture out into a flat cake and cook gently on one side for about 15 minutes.

3 Invert a large plate over the pan. Turn the cake out on to the plate and slide the uncooked side back into the pan to brown. Add the rest of the butter and cook for 10 more minutes, or until the cake is golden brown on both sides.

4 To serve, turn the cake out on to a plate, cut into wedges and serve immediately. Serve with red tomato salsa.

Deep-Fried Chèvre Wheels with Salad

SERVES 4

100g/4oz cylindrical-shaped chèvre
  (goat's cheese), without rind, chilled
1–2 large eggs, beaten
50–75g/2–3oz fresh breadcrumbs
1 cos lettuce (heart only) or 2 Little Gems
½ curly endive (heart only)
12 watercress sprigs
oil for deep-frying

Vinaigrette Dressing
2 tablespoons lemon juice
6 tablespoons extra-virgin olive oil
2 tablespoons walnut or hazelnut oil
salt and freshly ground pepper
pinch crushed dried chillies

1 Cut the chilled *chèvre* into 8 wheels or rounds 0.5cm/¼ inch thick. Dip the wheels in the beaten egg, draining carefully, and roll in the breadcrumbs, patting the coating on firmly. Chill until ready to use.

2 Wash and prepare the lettuce and curly endive. Wash the watercress sprigs. Shake the lettuce leaves, endive and watercress sprigs in a salad basket, or dry carefully with absorbent paper. Chill.

3 To make the dressing, combine the lemon juice, olive and walnut or hazelnut oil in a bowl. Season with salt, freshly ground black pepper and crushed dried chillies to taste, and beat until the mixture emulsifies.

4 Toss the lettuce leaves, endive and watercress sprigs separately in the vinaigrette.

5 When ready to serve, arrange the lettuce leaves around the edges of an oval serving platter, pile the endive in the centre, and scatter on individual salad plates.

6 Heat the oil in a deep-frier to 350°F/180°C, when a 2.5cm/1 inch cube of day-old bread will take 60 seconds to turn crisp and golden brown. Deep-fry the *chèvre* wheels in oil for 2 minutes or until golden brown. (Be careful not to allow the cheese to become too hot, or the breadcrumb coating will split.) Drain on absorbent paper.

7 To serve, arrange the *chèvre* wheels on the salad and serve immediately.

Grilled Polenta with Aubergine and Pesto

SERVES 4

4 tablespoons butter
4 tablespoons finely chopped onion
150g/6 oz 'instant' polenta
750ml/1¼ pints water
2 tablespoons butter
salt and freshly ground pepper
crushed dried chillies
olive oil for brushing

4 1cm/½ inch rounds unpeeled aubergine
(cut from the centre of a large aubergine)
chilled prepared pesto from an Italian
provisions store (or 1 jar of commercial
pesto, thickened with a little drained
Greek yogurt)
8 leaves fresh basil, cut into slivers

1   Prepare the polenta well ahead. In a medium saucepan, melt the butter; add the finely chopped onion and cook, stirring, until the onion is transparent. Add the water and bring to a fast simmer. Trickle in the polenta in a thin stream, stirring all the while. Bring the contents of the saucepan slowly to the boil again, then reduce the heat and let it simmer for 5 minutes, stirring constantly. Beat in the butter and add the salt, freshly ground pepper and crushed dried chillies, to taste.

2   Pour the mixture into 4 oiled individual pastry tins (with loose bottoms to facilitate removing the polenta rounds) or into an oiled rectangular baking tin. Allow mixture to cool.

3   When ready to grill the polenta, turn the polenta cakes out of the individual pastry tins (or, using a 10 or 12cm/4 or 5 inch pastry cutter, cut 4 rounds of polenta from the rectangular baking tin.

4   Brush each aubergine round with olive oil on both sides and place on a grid under the preheated grill. Brush each polenta round with oil and cook (with the aubergine rounds) under the preheated grill until a light crust forms; carefully turn the polenta and aubergine rounds and grill the other side.

5   To serve, place 1 round of grilled polenta on each heated plate; place l grilled round of aubergine on each polenta round; top each with a quenelle of pesto (made by shaping Italian pesto into an even egg shape, using 2 tablespoons to form the egg), and sprinkle the pesto with slivered basil leaves. Serve immediately.

If the pesto you are using is too liquid for this operation, mix it with a little drained Greek yogurt to solidify the mixture. Proceed as above.

Roasted Goat's Cheese with Soy and Lime Dressing

SERVES 4

4 fat slices beefsteak tomato	***Soy and Lime Dressing***
2–3 tablespoons olive oil	*4 tablespoons olive oil*
salt and freshly ground pepper	*2 tablespoons lime juice*
4 little round chèvre (goat's) cheeses	*4 teaspoons soy sauce*
	crushed dried chillies

1   Place 1 slice of tomato in each of 4 round ramekin (or egg) dishes. Brush with olive oil and season with salt and freshly ground pepper. Top each tomato slice with a round goat's cheese. Brush with olive oil and place in the preheated oven (190°C/ 375°F/Gas 5) for 10–15 minutes, or until the cheeses are golden brown and meltingly soft in the centre.

2   To make the dressing, combine the olive oil, lime juice, soy sauce and crushed dried chillies, to taste in a small bowl. Mix well.

3   Remove ramekins from the oven, spoon over the dressing and serve immediately.

Grilled Polenta with Aubergine and Pesto (see p.102)

Roasted Goat's Cheese with Soy and Lime Dressing (see p.103)

Vegetable Main Courses

Chinese Butternut Pumpkin with Ginger Pineapple Marinade

SERVES 6

900g/2lb butternut pumpkin
6 large pieces of preserved stem ginger

Ginger Pineapple Marinade
6 tablespoons soy sauce
6 tablespoons pineapple juice

2 teaspoons finely chopped root ginger
1 garlic clove, finely chopped
1 teaspoon dry mustard
4 tablespoons sake or dry sherry
1 tablespoon peanut oil
½ teaspoon curry powder

1 Peel the pumpkin, cut into 2.5cm/1 inch cubes, and place in a large bowl.

2 To make the ginger marinade, combine all the ingredients in a bowl and mix well. Pour the marinade over the pumpkin, mix well, and leave to marinate in the refrigerator for at least 4 hours, preferably overnight.

3 When ready to cook, heat the grill to medium. Cut the stem ginger into thin slices. Thread the pumpkin on to 6 skewers, alternating with ginger slices, and brush with marinade. Grill for about 10 minutes until the pumpkin is cooked through, turning the skewers and basting frequently with marinade. Serve immediately with boiled rice.

Stuffed Aubergine 'Imam Bayeldi'

SERVES 6

3 aubergines, weighing 225g/8oz each
salt
1 large Spanish onion, thinly sliced
225g/8oz can tomatoes, drained and
   chopped
3 tablespoons finely chopped parsley

¼ teaspoon sugar
freshly ground pepper
8–10 tablespoons olive oil
6 large garlic cloves
juice of 1 lemon

1 Wipe the aubergines with a damp cloth. Leaving about 1cm/½ inch of the stalk intact, peel away the leaves. Peel the aubergines lengthways into 1cm/½ inch wide strips. Leaving alternate strips of peel intact. Cut the aubergines in half lengthways and make deep slashes in the cut surface with a knife, about 2.5cm/1 inch apart, taking great care not to pierce through to the other side.

2 Sprinkle the thinly sliced onion with salt and allow to mellow for 30 minutes. Rinse thoroughly in warm water and squeeze dry in a cloth. Combine the onions in a bowl with the chopped tomatoes, 2 tablespoons finely chopped parsley and the sugar, and season with salt and freshly ground pepper to taste.

3 Preheat the oven to 170°C/325°F/Gas 3.

4 Pour 2–4 tablespoons olive oil into a shallow, heatproof casserole. Arrange the aubergine halves in the casserole, cut sides up. Cover each half with the tomato mixture, stuffing the mixture into the slashes and piling the rest on top. Lay a garlic clove on each half, and pour 1 tablespoon olive oil over each. Sprinkle with lemon juice.

5 Pour in enough water to come half-way up the sides of the aubergines. Bring to the boil, transfer casserole to the preheated oven and cook for 50 minutes, or until tender.

6 Just before serving, carefully transfer the aubergine halves to a deep serving dish. Remove the garlic cloves, sprinkle with the remaining finely chopped parsley, and pour some of the cooking juices around them.

Mediterranean Chargrilled Vegetables

SERVES 6–8

2 red peppers
2 green peppers
2 yellow peppers
1 red onion
1 aubergine
2 fennel roots
3 small to medium green courgettes
3 small to medium yellow courgettes
4 small carrots

Dressing
8 tablespoons olive oil
½–1 teaspoon soy sauce
1–2 tablespoons balsamic vinegar

1 garlic clove, finely chopped
½–1 teaspoon finely chopped ginger
1–2 teaspoons finely chopped onion
pinch of saffron
salt and freshly ground pepper

Garnish
(Three or more of the following)
6–8 blanched fine green beans
6–8 blanched baby sprouts
6–8 blanched mangetout
6–8 lightly steamed asparagus tips
½ packet of alfalfa shoots
½ can chick peas

1 Make the dressing by combining all the ingredients in a small bowl.

2 Cut the peppers in half, remove the seeds and cut into thick strips. Peel the onion and slice into rings. Cut the aubergine into slices. Trim the fennel roots and cut into strips. Top and tail the courgettes and cut into slices lengthways. Peel the carrots and cut into slices lengthways. Blanch the fennel strips and carrot slices. Drain.

3 Using a table-top chargrill or, if cooking outside, a barbecue, heat it until it is glowing red. Put on the onion slices and the red pepper strips and brush with the dressing. Cook, turning occasionally, and brush with more dressing when necessary. Then add the fennel, courgettes and carrots, brush with dressing and cook until all the vegetables are marked on both sides by the grill and are crisp.

4 To serve, place the vegetables on an oval serving dish and garnish with your choice of blanched green beans, sprouts, mangetout, steamed asparagus tips, alfalfa shoots and drained chick peas. Serve with olive bread, spread with tapenade (puréed olive paste), and have a bowl of extra dressing to add if required. Chargrilled vegetables are even more delicious served cold the next day.

Blanquette of Vegetables

SERVES 4

Your choice of 5 or more of the following vegetables:
16 mangetouts, trimmed
16 spring onions, white parts only (reserve green parts for garnish)
16 baby carrots, trimmed
16 baby corn
16 button mushrooms, wiped clean, with stems trimmed
16 button onions, peeled
16 broccoli florets
16 small new potatoes, peeled
100g/4oz fresh peas, removed from the pod
4 green (or 1 yellow) courgette(s), trimmed and cut into 2.5cm/1 inch segments

asparagus spears, trimmed to 5cm/2 inch lengths

Blanquette sauce
2½ tablespoons butter
2½ tablespoons flour
1 crumbled vegetable stock cube
600ml/1 pint double cream,
salt and freshly ground pepper
lemon juice

Vegetable poaching liquid
50g/2oz butter
300ml/½ pint water
½ vegetable stock cube

1   Prepare the blanquette sauce. In the top of a double saucepan (or in a stainless steel bowl set inside a heatproof saucepan) over simmering water, melt the butter. Add the flour and continue to cook, stirring constantly, until the butter and flour are well mixed. Stir in the crumbled vegetable stock cube and add the double cream gradually, stirring, until the sauce is well mixed. Continue to cook over simmering water until the sauce has reduced to half the original quantity. Add salt, freshly ground pepper and lemon juice to taste, and strain into a clean saucepan for later use.

2   Meanwhile, prepare the vegetable poaching liquid. In a small saucepan, combine the butter, water and ½ vegetable stock cube and bring gently to the boil, stirring constantly, to blend the ingredients. Remove from the heat and set aside.

3   Blanch 5 (or more) varieties of vegetables of your choice by putting them in a saucepan with cold water to cover and bringing them gently to the boil. Remove the vegetables from the pan with a slotted spoon.

4   When ready to serve, bring the vegetable poaching liquid to the boil in a shallow heatproof saucepan. Add the blanched vegetables and cook over a gentle heat until they are crisp-tender. Bring the blanquette sauce to the boil, add the poached vegetables, and warm through. Serve immediately.

Vegetable Charlotte

SERVES 4–6

1 large onion, finely chopped
2 garlic cloves, finely chopped
2 tablespoons olive oil
4 tablespoons butter
700g/1½lb aubergines, diced
1 teaspoon dried thyme
1–1½ teaspoons soy sauce
salt and freshly ground pepper
crushed dried chillies
150ml/¼ pint white wine
300ml/½ pt vegetable stock
4–6 tablespoons tomato purée

8 tablespoons cooked rice
1 tablespoon cornflour
225g/8oz frozen mixed vegetables
melted butter
5 slices white bread
4 tablespoons freshly grated Parmesan
4 tablespoons breadcrumbs

Vegetable casing
225g/8oz each of carrots, potatoes
and fine French beans

1 Preheat the oven to 180°C/350°F/Gas 4. Sauté the onion and garlic in the oil and butter until transparent. Remove the vegetables with a slotted spoon and reserve. Add the diced aubergines, thyme, soy sauce, and salt, ground pepper and crushed dried chillies to taste, and sauté stirring constantly, until browned. Remove from the heat.

2 In a small saucepan, combine the wine, stock and tomato purée and cook until reduced by half. Add to the aubergine with the reserved garlic and onions, and simmer, covered, for 10 minutes. Stir in the rice, and cornflour mixed with 4 tablespoons water and simmer for 3 minutes more. Stir the mixed vegetables into the mixture.

3 To make the striped vegetable casing, cut the carrots and potatoes into thin sticks (same diameter as the fine French beans) as tall as a 1.1 litre/2 pint charlotte mould. Trim the French beans to fit. Blanch the vegetables.

4 To assemble the charlotte, butter the mould, cut the bread into triangles and line the bottom. Brush with melted butter. Line the sides of the mould with the vegetable sticks. Fill with the vegetable mixture. Top with grated cheese and crumbs.

5 Place a roasting tin over a high heat on the top of the stove, half fill with boiling water, place the filled charlotte mould in the centre of the tin and wait until the water comes to the boil again before carefully transferring the roasting tin and charlotte to the preheated oven. Bake for 45 minutes. Remove the bain-marie (roasting tin) from the oven and set aside. Unmould carefully, and serve with mashed potatoes.

Braised Courgettes with Savoury Vegetable Stuffing

SERVES 4

8 large courgettes
salt
3 tablespoons olive oil
1 small onion, finely chopped
50g/2oz finely diced red pepper
50g/2oz finely diced green pepper
25g/1oz finely diced celery
50g/2oz finely diced tomato
1 tablespoon capers, finely chopped
100g/4oz fresh white breadcrumbs
2 tablespoons finely chopped parsley
1 teaspoon dried thyme
1 tablespoon lemon juice

freshly ground pepper
1 medium egg, beaten
butter
sprigs of parsley

Cheese Sauce
25g/1oz butter
25g/1oz flour
300ml/10fl oz hot milk
100g/4oz Cheddar cheese, grated
pinch of grated nutmeg
salt and freshly ground pepper

1   Preheat the oven to 190°C/375°F/Gas 5.

2   Hollow out the centres of the courgettes (using an apple corer) from each end. Boil the hollowed-out courgettes in salted water for 5 minutes to soften them. Drain thoroughly and pat dry with absorbent paper.

3   Heat the olive oil in a frying pan. Add the finely chopped onion and fry for 5 minutes until soft. Remove from the heat and stir in the finely diced peppers, celery, tomato, capers, breadcrumbs, finely chopped parsley, thyme and lemon juice. Season with salt and freshly ground pepper to taste, then bind all the ingredients together with the beaten egg.

4 Carefully stuff the hollowed-out courgettes with the filling. Arrange in a lightly buttered dish, cover with foil and bake in the preheated oven for 30 minutes.

5 To make cheese sauce, melt the butter in a saucepan and stir in the flour, using a wooden spoon. Cook over a moderate heat for 2 minutes, then remove from the heat. Add the milk gradually, stirring until thick and smooth. Add the grated cheese, nutmeg, and salt and freshly ground pepper to taste. Heat until the cheese has melted into the sauce.

6 Remove the courgettes from the oven and divide them between 4 plates. Pour a little of the sauce over each serving and garnish with sprigs of parsley.

Creamed Country Vegetables

SERVES 4

700g/1½lb green beans
salt
8-12 medium carrots
6 tablespoons vegetable stock
2 tablespoons caster sugar

6 spring onions, cut into 1cm/½ inch segments
3 tablespoons double cream
freshly ground pepper
1 tablespoon finely chopped chervil
1 tablespoon finely chopped parsley

1 Trim and wash the green beans and cut them into 5cm/2 inch lengths. Cook in a large saucepan of boiling salted water, uncovered, for 3–4 minutes or until the beans are tender but still firm. Drain and refresh under cold running water.

2 Peel or scrape the carrots and cut into thirds crosswise.

3 In a saucepan, simmer the vegetable stock, caster sugar, carrots and spring onion segments together for 10 minutes or until the carrots are tender but still firm.

4 Toss the beans, carrots and onion in the cream over a low heat for 1–2 minutes to reheat. Season with salt and freshly ground pepper to taste, and serve in a heated dish sprinkled with the finely chopped chervil and parsley.

Peking Aubergine

SERVES 4

3 tablespoons Chinese plum sauce
2 tablespoons clear honey
1–2 tablespoons Chinese hoisin sauce
¼ teaspoon Chinese chilli sauce
sesame oil
23cm/9 inch piece of cucumber
5 spring onions

Chinese pancakes (allow at least 4
  per person)
2 aubergines
sesame seeds
plain flour
olive oil
soy sauce

1 First make the traditional Peking duck sauce by mixing together the plum sauce, clear honey, hoisin sauce and chilli sauce with 2 tablespoons sesame oil. Put this mixture into a small Chinese serving bowl. Cut the cucumber and spring onions into thin strips about 7cm/3 inches long and put into 2 other serving bowls.

2 Brush the pancakes on either side with sesame oil and put them into a steamer basket ready for steaming. Quarter fill a pan (the right size to hold the steamer basket), with water, and bring to simmering point.

3 While this is heating, cut the aubergines crosswise into 0.5cm/¼ inch thick slices, then slice into 'fingers' about 7cm/3 inches long. Take two shallow bowls and put sesame seeds into one and plain flour into the other. Coat the aubergine fingers (in batches) first with the sesame seeds and then with the flour.

4 In a frying pan, heat a little oil to sizzling point, add the aubergine fingers, and allow to cook until they are golden on all sides. Pour a little soy sauce into the pan and shake the pan vigorously until the aubergine fingers are well coated. Transfer to a heated serving bowl and keep warm. Steam the pancakes for 2–3 minutes and turn out on to a warmed plate, separating them as you do this.

5 To assemble the Peking aubergine rolled pancake (guests assemble their own): place some cucumber and onion strips in the centre of the pancake; add two or three aubergine fingers, a spoonful of Peking duck sauce and roll up. Eat with chopsticks or, more simply, with your fingers.

Vietnamese Spring Rolls

SERVES 4

4 courgettes
2–3 tablespoons olive oil
4–6 Shiitake mushrooms,
  finely chopped
100g/4oz beansprouts
½ teaspoon soy sauce
2 tablespoons dry sherry
½–1 teaspoon chopped ginger
salt and freshly ground pepper
8 spring roll wrappers (see below)

1 egg, beaten
oil
8 black olives
4 sprigs of fresh coriander
soy sauce flavoured with lime juice
  and crushed dried chillies

To serve
boiled rice
curly endive

1   Wipe the courgettes, trim and cut into small batons.

2   Heat the olive oil in a large frying pan. Add the chopped mushrooms, sprouts and courgettes and cook for 1–2 minutes until the vegetables have softened slightly. Add the soy sauce, dry sherry and chopped ginger and season with salt and freshly ground pepper to taste.

3   Put 2 tablespoons of the vegetable mixture at the top end of a spring roll wrapper and roll up, folding in the ends and brushing the surface with beaten egg as you roll. Repeat with the remaining wrappers to make 8 spring rolls. (If using filo pastry, cut each sheet in half.)

4   Heat the oil in a deep-fat frier to 180°C/350°F, or until a cube of stale bread dropped into the oil turns brown in 60 seconds. Deep-fry the spring rolls for 1–2 minutes or until golden brown, and drain on absorbent paper. Transfer 2 spring rolls to each of 4 individual serving plates and garnish with black olives and sprigs of fresh coriander. Serve with accompanying small bowls of soy sauce which you have flavoured with lime juice and crushed dried chillies. Serve with boiled rice and curly endive.

If you have difficulty buying spring roll wrappers (which are available from Chinese delicatessens), use filo pastry instead.

7 Vegetable Couscous

SERVES 4–6

1.2 litres/2 pints vegetable
stock, made with stock cubes
paprika
cumin
cinnamon
cayenne
ground ginger
saffron
2 medium-sized potatoes

4 small turnips
1 swede
4 parsnips
6 small carrots
6 small courgettes
2 red peppers
1 packet couscous
butter, softened
salt

1–2 tablespoons freshly
grated Parmesan cheese

Garnish
1 can chick peas, drained
1 Spanish onion, sliced
butter
6 tablespoons raisins,
plumped in water

1 Put the vegetable stock in the base of a large saucepan which has a steamer that
fits tightly over the top and add ½ teaspoon each of paprika and cumin and
cinnamon, a pinch each of cayenne and ground ginger and 2 good pinches of saffron.
Bring to simmering point over a medium heat.

2 Peel the potatoes and cut into 6 wedges. Peel the turnips and cut in half. Peel the
swede and cut into the same size wedges as the potatoes. Peel the parsnips and cut in
half lengthways. Peel the carrots and leave whole. Top and tail the courgettes. Cut
the peppers into quarters and deseed. Add potatoes, turnips, swedes and parsnips to
the stock and simmer for 15–20 minutes. Then add carrots, peppers and courgettes.

3 Line the steamer with a large piece of wet muslin or a wet tea towel. Add the
couscous to the lined steamer, place the steamer on the pan over the boiling stock,
cover and steam the couscous for 20 minutes. To finish, tip the couscous from the
steamer on to a board or work surface and, using your fingers, work in a knob of
softened butter and a pinch or two of salt, paprika, cumin, cinnamon, ground ginger
and cayenne. Add freshly grated Parmesan and rub gently through the couscous.
Return the couscous to the steamer, and cover and steam for a further 10 minutes.

4 Heat the chick peas in a small saucepan and keep warm. In a frying pan sauté the
sliced onion in 2 tablespoons of butter until soft. Keep warm.

5 Pile the couscous on to a heated serving dish. Arrange the strained vegetables
decoratively around the sides and top of the couscous. Garnish with chick peas,
raisins and sautéd onion. Serve immediately, with an accompanying bowl of the
highly flavoured stock as a sauce.

Gratin of Colcannon with Glazed Vegetable Strips

SERVES 4

450g/1lb cabbage	freshly ground pepper
4–6 potatoes	crushed dried chillies
salt	150ml/¼ pint double cream
4–6 young carrots	2 egg yolks
4–6 young long turnips	4 tablespoons fresh breadcrumbs
butter	4 tablespoons freshly grated cheese (optional)
½ vegetable stock cube, crumbled	

1 Preheat the oven to 190°C/375°F/Gas 5.

2 Remove the outer leaves from the cabbage, wash, quarter and core. Peel the potatoes. Cook the quartered cabbage and the potatoes in salted water until tender. Drain.

3 Peel and slice the carrots and turnips into thin strips. Put into a saucepan of salted water (enough to cover) and blanch. Pour off the water.

4 Add 4 tablespoons each of butter and water to the pan together with the crumbled vegetable stock cube, and simmer the carrots and turnips until tender. Season with salt, freshly ground pepper and crushed dried chillies to taste.

5 Chop the cabbage finely, put it in a bowl with the potatoes and mash until smooth. Combine with the double cream, egg yolks and 2 tablespoons butter and season with salt and freshly ground pepper to taste.

6 Spread half the cabbage mixture in the bottom of a well-buttered heatproof gratin dish. Arrange a layer of alternating strips of carrot and turnip down the centre and cover with the remaining cabbage mixture. Sprinkle with the breadcrumbs, top with a little freshly grated cheese, if desired, dot with butter, and cook in the preheated oven for 30 minutes or until golden.

Chick Pea Fritters with Watercress (or Corn) Salad

SERVES 8 (MAKES ABOUT 60 FRITTERS)

2 x 400g/14oz cans chick peas
2 slices white bread, crusts removed
4 garlic cloves, chopped
4 tablespoons chopped parsley
50g/2oz burghul (cracked wheat),
* rinsed and drained*

1 teaspoon ground coriander seeds
1 teaspoon cumin
½ teaspoon freshly ground pepper
½ teaspoon cayenne pepper
2 teaspoons salt
vegetable oil

1 Drain and rinse the chick peas and grind them in a food processor or blender until smooth.

2 Soak the bread in water and squeeze it dry. Chop the bread with the chopped garlic and parsley and combine with the chick peas. Add the burghul, spices and salt and mix thoroughly. Leave the mixture in a cool place for at least 1 hour.

3 Shape the mixture with wet hands into small balls, about 2.5cm/1 inch in diameter.

4 In a deep-fat frier, preferably one with a basket, heat the oil until very hot, about 180°C/350°F, or until a cube of stale bread dropped into the oil turns brown in 60 seconds. Fry the fritters, a few at a time, for 2–3 minutes.

5 Serve with a watercress or corn salad, dressed with a well-flavoured vinaigrette.

Mushroom Ratatouille

SERVES 6–8

350g/12oz medium-sized button
mushrooms
100g/4oz wild or Shiitake mushrooms
2 large red peppers
2 large yellow peppers
2 large green peppers
2 large courgettes
olive oil
1 medium-sized onion, finely chopped
2 garlic cloves, finely chopped

1 tablespoon fresh coriander leaves, chopped
ground ginger
cayenne
2 teaspoons soy sauce
salt and freshly ground pepper
Herbes de Provence

Garnish
chopped fresh coriander, basil or
flat-leaf parsley

1 Wash the mushrooms. Remove the stalks and cut the caps in half (horizontally) to make 2 even-sized rounds. Trim the wild or Shiitake mushrooms and wipe clean.

2 Cut the peppers in half, remove the seeds and trim the membranes. Using a small round pastry cutter, cut rounds out of the peppers so that they are roughly the same diameter as the mushrooms. Cut the courgettes into 0.5cm/¼ inch thick rounds.

3 Heat 2 tablespoons olive oil in a large heavy-based frying pan and add the pepper rounds. Add the finely chopped onion and garlic and allow to cook for 2 minutes. Add the chopped coriander, a pinch each of ginger and cayenne, and cook over a low heat, stirring gently, until the onion is translucent. Transfer the mixture to a plate and keep warm.

4 Clean the pan. Add a little more olive oil and sauté the mushrooms, stirring for several minutes. Add 2 teaspoons soy sauce. Stir well and allow to cook for another minute. Then add the sliced courgettes and cook for a further couple of minutes, or until the courgettes are tender but still crisp.

5 Return the pepper mixture to the pan with the mushrooms and courgettes. Season with salt, freshly ground pepper and a sprinkling of Herbs of Provence, and briefly sauté the whole mixture until warmed through.

6 Serve immediately, garnished with a few chopped fresh herbs such as coriander and parsley.

Roasted Pepper, Tomato and Egg Salad with Garlic and Herb Dressing

SERVES 6

2 garlic cloves, finely chopped	*salt and freshly ground pepper*
1–2 tablespoons each finely chopped	*2 large green peppers*
parsley, tarragon, chervil	*2 large red peppers*
and chives	*6 firm tomatoes*
6–8 tablespoons olive oil	*6 hard-boiled eggs*
2 tablespoons red wine vinegar	*24 black olives*

1 Preheat the grill to high.

2 Prepare a herb dressing by combining the finely chopped garlic and herbs with the olive oil and wine vinegar. Season with salt and freshly ground pepper to taste.

3 Place the peppers under the preheated grill as close to the heat as possible. Cook, turning the peppers continually, until the skin on all sides has charred. Rub the skin off under cold running water. Cut the peppers in strips, 4–6 to each pepper, keeping the colours separate. Wash off the seeds and excess fibre. Drain on absorbent paper.

4 Slice the tomatoes thickly and cover the bottom of a flat serving dish with the slices. Sprinkle with a quarter of the herb dressing, add a layer of green pepper slices and sprinkle with more dressing. Add a layer of red pepper slices and sprinkle with dressing.

5 Slice the hard-boiled eggs into rings and cover the red pepper slices with a layer of egg slices. Pour over the remaining dressing. Garnish with black olives and chill for at least 30 minutes before serving.

Potato, Apple and Walnut Salad with Celery

SERVES 4

4 boiled new potatoes
4 red-skinned apples
juice of 2 lemons
4 sticks of celery, sliced

50g/2oz walnuts, halved
mayonnaise or French dressing
lettuce leaves

1 Peel and dice the potatoes. Core and dice the apples and sprinkle with lemon juice.

2 Combine the diced potatoes and apples in a bowl with the sliced celery and walnut halves, and toss together in mayonnaise or French dressing (according to taste).

3 Pile the mixture into a salad bowl lined with lettuce leaves.

My Ratatouille

SERVES 4

6 tablespoons olive oil
2 Spanish onions, sliced
2 green peppers, seeded and sliced
2 large garlic cloves, crushed
2 aubergines, cut into diamonds
2 courgettes, cut into 1cm/½inch slices

4–6 ripe tomatoes, peeled, seeded and
   cut into wedges
salt and freshly ground pepper
2 tablespoons chopped parsley
pinch or two of dried herbes de provence

1 Heat 2 tablespoons olive oil in a thick-bottomed saucepan. Add the sliced onions and peppers and sauté until transparent. Lower heat and continue to cook the vegetables for 5 more minutes, stirring from time to time. Transfer the vegetables to a large bowl and reserve.

2 Add 2 tablespoons olive oil to the pan. Add the crushed garlic and diced aubergines and cook for 5 minutes. Remove and reserve. Add 2 tablespoons olive oil and add the courgette slices and tomato wedges, then cook for 5 minutes. Return all the reserved vegetables to the pan. Season with salt and freshly ground pepper to taste, chopped parsley, dried *herbes de provence* or dried marjoram or oregano and heat through. Serve immediately.

Flat Soufflé Omelette with Green Herbs

SERVES 4-6

150g/6oz fresh spinach (or Little Gem lettuce or mâche leaves)

1–2 tablespoons chopped green onion

½ garlic clove, finely chopped

extra-virgin oil

salt and freshly ground pepper

4 tablespoons chopped chives

2 tablespoons chopped basil, plus 6 basil leaves

2 tablespoons chopped mint, plus 6 mint leaves

2 tablespoons tarragon leaves, plus 6 tender tarragon tops

2–4 tablespoons chopped fennel, plus 6 tender fennel tops

2–4 egg yolks

4-6 tablespoons crème fraîche

6 tablespoons freshly grated Gruyère cheese

6–8 egg whites

Uncooked Tomato Sauce

6 beefsteak tomatoes, peeled, seeded and diced

extra-virgin olive oil

salt and crushed dried chillies

1 Blanch the spinach or lettuce leaves in lightly salted boiling water. Drain and press dry. Chop finely.

2 In a medium-sized frying pan, sauté the chopped onion and garlic in 2 tablespoons olive oil until the vegetables are transparent. Add the finely chopped spinach and continue to cook, stirring, for 1 minute. Season with salt, freshly ground pepper and crushed dried chillies to taste. Add the chopped chives, basil and mint and sauté, stirring constantly, for 1 more minute. Drain off excess oil and reserve.

3 In a medium-sized bowl, whisk the egg yolks, *crème fraîche* and grated Gruyère until well blended. Stir in the spinach and herb mixture and reserve.

4 To make the sauce, combine the peeled, seeded and diced tomatoes in a bowl with olive oil and salt and crushed dried chillies to taste. Chill for 2 hours before serving.

5 When ready to cook the omelette, beat the egg whites until stiff in a clean bowl – using a clean electric beater. Fold them gently into the creamy herb and egg yolk mixture and pour into a buttered frying pan. Cook over a medium heat, adding a little more oil or butter if necessary, for 4 minutes. Place a large plate over the omelette and turn it over on the plate. Slide the omelette back into the pan and continue to cook for a few minutes more, or until it is golden brown on the other side.

6 Garnish with the whole herb leaves and serve immediately, accompanied by the chilled uncooked tomato sauce.

Aubergine and Red Pepper Spiedini

SERVES 4

125ml/4fl oz olive oil
1 tablespoon finely chopped fresh rosemary
1 tablespoon finely chopped garlic
1–2 teaspoons finely grated lemon zest
salt and freshly ground pepper
crushed dried chillies
1 unpeeled aubergine (450–550g/1–1 ¼lb)
32 (2.5cm/1 inch) squares red peppers
  (2–3 red peppers)

8 small bamboo skewers, soaked in water for
  30 minutes
4 15cm/6 inch pieces French baguette,
  halved lengthwise

Garnish
Tomato slices
Spring onion segments (green part only)
Sprigs of fresh rosemary

1 In a small bowl, combine the olive oil, chopped rosemary, garlic and lemon zest. Season with salt, freshly ground pepper and crushed dried chillies to taste. Divide the mixture between 2 bowls – 1 medium-sized one to marinate the pepper squares for 1 hour at room temperature; and 1 smaller one (covered with plastic wrap) to keep in the refrigerator until you are ready to use it to glaze the cooked spiedini.

2 When ready to cook, preheat the oven to 200°C/400°F/Gas 6. Cut the unpeeled aubergine into 24 cubes, each 2.5 x 2.5cm/1 inch x 1 inch square. Alternate 4 pepper squares and 3 aubergine cubes on each skewer. Arrange on a large baking sheet. Place the bread, cut side up, on the sheet. Brush the vegetable skewers and bread with some of the reserved dressing. Bake the skewers and bread for 5–6 minutes. Turn the skewers over and bake the skewers and bread until the vegetables are brown and just cooked through, about 4–6 more minutes.

3 To serve, place 1 toast on each plate and place 2 skewers on each toast. Brush lightly with the remaining reserved dressing. Garnish each plate with tomato slices, spring onion segments and sprigs of fresh rosemary.

Mushrooms in Madeira

SERVES 4-6

butter
1½ tablespoons plain flour
1 vegetable stock cube
1 tablespoon tomato purée
600ml/1 pint whipping cream
cayenne pepper
salt and freshly ground pepper
ground nutmeg
225g/8oz large button mushrooms
225g/8oz small button mushrooms

2 tablespoons finely chopped shallots
1 glass each of dry white wine and Madeira

Garnish (optional)
8 lightly cooked broccoli florets
8 cherry tomatoes
A few small wild mushrooms
  (ceps, chanterelles if possible)
Finely chopped flat-leafed parsley

1   In a bowl (or saucepan) over simmering water, melt 1½ tablespoons butter. When it is bubbling, stir in the flour and cook for a couple of minutes. Crumble in the stock cube and stir until it is incorporated into the butter and flour mixture. Add the tomato purée and mix well. Using a whisk, whip in the cream and add a pinch of cayenne, salt and freshly ground pepper and a little freshly ground nutmeg to taste. Cook, stirring constantly, until the mixture thickens, and leave over a gentle heat.

2   Heat 2 tablespoons of butter in a frying pan and add the trimmed button mushrooms. Sauté for a few minutes, stirring to coat the mushrooms on all sides with butter. Add a little water and continue to cook over a high heat until the water has evaporated and the mushrooms are glazed. Remove from the heat and reserve.

3   In a small saucepan melt 2 tablespoons of butter and add the chopped shallots. Cook until they start to turn translucent, then add the Madeira and boil until the liquid is reduced to 2–3 tablespoonfuls. Pour this mixture into the tomato cream sauce. In the same saucepan sauté the wild mushrooms (if you have them) until tender. Remove the mushrooms and keep warm. Add the dry white wine to the pan and boil until the liquid is reduced to 2–3 tablespoonfuls. Add to the sauce.

4   In another frying pan heat 2 tablespoons of butter and, over a medium heat, sauté the cherry tomatoes and broccoli florets, sizzling until golden on all sides. Keep warm.

5   When ready to serve, re-heat the button mushrooms and arrange on a heated serving plate. Spoon over the sauce and garnish with the wild mushrooms, tomatoes and broccoli, and chopped fresh herbs.

Spinach Salad with Beetroot and White Beans

SERVES 4–6

450g/1lb young spinach leaves
½ a small onion, thinly sliced
salt
6–8 tablespoons olive oil
2 tablespoons red wine vinegar
½ teaspoon Dijon mustard

1 garlic clove, finely chopped
2 tablespoons finely chopped parsley
freshly ground pepper
4 small pickled beetroots, thinly sliced
400g/14oz can haricots blancs, drained

1 Wash the spinach several times in cold water. Drain. Remove the coarse stems and any yellowed or damaged leaves. Chill.

2 Soak the thinly sliced onion in salted iced water for 10 minutes. Drain.

3 Combine the olive oil and red wine vinegar. Add the Dijon mustard, finely chopped garlic and parsley and season with salt and freshly ground pepper to taste.

4 Arrange the spinach leaves in a salad bowl. Pour over the dressing and toss until each leaf glistens. Garnish with the thinly sliced onion and beetroot and the *haricots blancs*.

Lentil Supper Salad

SERVES 4–6

250g/8oz lentils
1 Spanish onion, finely chopped
6 tablespoons olive oil
1 garlic clove
1 bay leaf
salt
2 tablespoons wine vinegar
freshly ground pepper
crushed dried chillies
tomato wedges
black olives

Dressing
½ Spanish onion, finely chopped
4 tablespoons finely chopped parsley
1 teaspoon prepared mustard
½ vegetable stock cube, crumbled
salt and freshly ground pepper
6–8 tablespoons olive oil
juice of ½ lemon

1 Soak the lentils overnight in water to cover. Drain.

2 Sauté the finely chopped onion in 2 tablespoons olive oil until transparent. Add the garlic clove, bay leaf, 1 teaspoon salt and 1.3 litres/2½ pints water and simmer the lentils in this stock for about 2 hours or until tender. Drain and cool. Remove the garlic clove and bay leaf. Add the remaining olive oil and the wine vinegar and season with salt, freshly ground pepper and crushed dried chillies, to taste.

3 To make the dressing, combine the finely chopped onion and parsley, prepared mustard and crumbled vegetable stock cube in a bowl and season with salt and freshly ground pepper, to taste. Mix well. Pour the olive oil, little by little, into the mixture, beating continuously, until the sauce thickens. Flavour with lemon juice.

4 Pour the dressing over the lentils, mix thoroughly, and garnish with tomato wedges and black olives.

Middle Eastern Bread Salad

SERVES 4–6

4 pitta bread
olive oil
lemon juice
salt
1 cucumber, peeled, seeded and diced
4 tomatoes, seeded and diced
1 red pepper, seeded and diced
1 yellow pepper, seeded and diced
1 avocado, peeled, pitted and diced
12 Greek or Cyprus black olives, pitted
   and halved
½ can drained chick peas

8 cos lettuce leaves cut into 2.5cm/1 inch slices
4 spring onions (green parts only), sliced
sprigs of fresh coriander
sprigs of fresh basil
sprigs of fresh flat-leafed parsley

Vinaigrette Dressing
6–8 tablespoons extra-virgin olive oil
2 tablespoons lemon juice
1–2 garlic cloves, finely chopped
salt and freshly ground pepper
pinch of crushed dried chillies

1   Preheat the oven to 400°C/200°F/Gas 6. Separate the rounds of pitta bread by inserting the point of a sharp knife and opening up each slice horizontally. Stack 2 sides of each bread and cut into 2.5cm/1 inch squares. Continue with the remaining 3 breads.

2   In a shallow soup bowl, combine 6 tablespoons olive oil, 2 tablespoons lemon juice, and salt, to taste (as you would for a vinaigrette dressing). Toss the pitta squares lightly in this dressing. Then place the squares in a single layer on a baking sheet and bake until lightly toasted (about 5 minutes). Remove from the oven.

3   To make the dressing, combine the olive oil, lemon juice, finely chopped garlic and salt, freshly ground pepper and crushed dried chillies to taste. Mix well.

4   In a salad bowl, combine the diced cucumber, tomatoes, peppers and avocado. Add the halved black olives, chick peas and sliced lettuce and spring onions.

5   Separate the leaves from the sprigs of coriander, basil and flat-leafed parsley. Add the leaves to the salad, slicing the basil and parsley leaves coarsely if they are large.

6   Just before serving, pour the vinaigrette dressing over the salad, add the toasted pitta squares and toss lightly.

Peppered Aubergine Steaks

SERVES 4

1 large fat aubergine (700g/1 ½ lb)
2–3 tablespoons coarsely crushed
  black peppercorns
salt
4 tablespoons melted butter or olive oil
juice of ½ a lemon

2 tablespoons finely chopped parsley
8 thin slices of lemon

To Serve
tomato salsa

1 Heat the grill

2 Cut the large aubergine crosswise into 8 even slices (steaks) 2cm/¼ inch thick. Brush the steaks with half the melted butter or olive oil and sprinkle with the lemon juice.

3 Press the coarsely crushed black peppercorns into the flesh of the aubergine steaks on both sides with the heel of your hand, and sprinkle with salt to taste.

4 Grill the steaks about 10cm/4 inches from the heat for 8–10 minutes on each side, brushing with the remaining melted butter (or oil) when you turn them over.

5 When the steaks are done, place them on a heated serving dish and garnish with finely chopped parsley and lemon slices.

6 Serve with Red Tomato Salsa (see p. 219) and choice of vegetables.

Provençal Potato Brandade

SERVES 4

5 large potatoes
salt
6 thin lemon slices, halved
12 black olives

Aïoli sauce
4 garlic cloves, finely chopped
salt
2 medium egg yolks
250ml/9 fl oz olive oil
freshly ground pepper
juice of 1 lemon

1 Peel and wash the potatoes and cut into 2.5cm/1 inch dice. Boil in salted water until cooked, but still firm – about 15 minutes.

2 To make the Aïoli sauce, crush the finely chopped garlic to a smooth paste with a little salt, using a pestle and mortar or pressing it on a plate with a round bladed knife. Blend in the egg yolks until the mixture is smooth. Add the olive oil, drop by drop at first as you would for a mayonnaise, whisking constantly. Continue adding olive oil in a fine trickle, whisking continually. The Aïoli will thicken gradually until it reaches a stiff, firm consistency. Season with additional salt and freshly ground pepper to taste. Add the lemon juice.

3 Purée the cooked potatoes in a blender, adding the Aïoli. Turn the brandade into a bowl, cover with clingfilm and chill in the refrigerator overnight.

4 Just before serving, add more lemon juice if needed and freshly ground pepper, to taste. Mound the mixture in a salad bowl. Surround the brandade with a ring of halved lemon slices and place a black olive on each slice.

Provençal Grilled Vegetables

SERVES 4

4–8 slices unpeeled aubergine,
   0.5cm/¼ inch thick and 7–10cm/
   3–4 inches in diameter
4–8 slices sweet potato, 0.5cm/¼ inch
   thick and 7–10cm/3–4 inches in
   diameter
4–8 thick slices beefsteak tomato
   7–10cm/3–4 inches in diameter
olive oil
Herbes de Provence
salt and freshly ground pepper

Garnish
Pesto piping sauce: fresh pesto sauce mixed
   with a little cold mashed potato and/or
   drained Greek yogurt to make it of piping
   consistency.
Rouille piping sauce: canned pimento, puréed
   with a little mashed garlic and tomato
   purée, mixed with a little cold mashed
   potato and/or drained Greek yogurt to make
   it of piping consistency.
Saffron piping sauce: home-made mayonnaise
   flavoured with saffron and mixed with a
   little cold mashed potato and/or Greek
   yogurt to make it of piping consistency
black olives
sprigs of fresh basil

1 Preheat the grill for 20 minutes. Brush the aubergine, sweet potato and tomato slices on both sides with olive oil, and season generously with Herbes de Provence and salt and freshly ground pepper, to taste. Grill on the preheated grill for 5–6 minutes on each side, or until the vegetables are cooked through.

2 Transfer the vegetables to a heated serving dish and garnish with one or all of the following sauces: pesto, rouille and/or saffron mayonnaise, piped in decorative swirls on each vegetable. (see photograph opposite). Garnish with black olives and sprigs of fresh basil, if desired.

Mixed Vegetable Kebabs

SERVES 6 (MAKES 12 KEBABS)

3 aubergine slices, 2.5cm/1 inch thick	**Marinade**
12 courgette slices, 2.5cm/1 inch thick	6 tablespoons olive oil
12 little white onions	4 tablespoons dry sherry
¼ vegetable stock cube, crumbled	1–2 garlic cloves, finely chopped
melted butter	¼ of a Spanish onion, finely chopped
12 button mushrooms	2 tablespoons finely chopped parsley
3 thick cucumber slices, 2.5cm/1 inch thick	1 teaspoon dried oregano
	salt and freshly ground pepper
12 green or red pepper segments	pinch of crushed dried chillies

1 Combine the marinade ingredients in a mixing bowl.

2 Cut the aubergine slices into quarters and trim into 2.5–4cm/1–1¹/2 inch squares.
Place the aubergine squares, sliced courgettes and onions in a saucepan with the
crumbled vegetable stock cube and 3 tablespoons each of butter and water and
simmer the vegetables in this liquid, covered, for 5 minutes.

3 Wash the mushrooms and trim the stems.

4 Place the cucumber slices, pepper segments, aubergine, courgettes and onions in a
large flat bowl. Add the mushrooms. Spoon over the marinade, mix well, and chill for
2 hours.

5 Remove the vegetables from the marinade one by one, threading them alternately
on 12 metal or wooden skewers (2 skewers per person). Refrigerate until ready to
grill.

6 Heat the grill to high.

7 With a pastry brush, coat the kebabs with melted butter. Place them under the
preheated grill and grill for 6–8 minutes, turning frequently as they cook, so that the
vegetables do not burn.

Thai Vegetable Stir-Fry

SERVES 4–6

100g/4oz blanched carrots, sliced
100g/4oz blanched broccoli florets
100g/4oz blanched green beans
100g/4oz blanched mangetouts
1 red pepper, cut into strips, rounds
*   or arrow shapes*
1 green pepper, cut into strips, rounds
*   or arrow shapes*
4 sticks of celery, cut diagonally into
*   segments*

100g/4oz button mushrooms, washed
*   and stems trimmed*
4 spring onions, cut into 0.5cm/¹/4
*   inch segments*
4 tablespoons vegetable oil
1–2 tablespoons soy sauce
lemon juice
Tabasco sauce (or a pinch or two of
*   crushed dried chillies)*
pinch of sugar

1 Prepare all the vegetables before you start cooking by cutting them all to size, blanching those that require it by putting them in cold water to cover and bringing them slowly to the boil, then draining.

2 Place the raw and blanched vegetables into individual bowls near the cooker (you won't have time, once you start cooking, to chop or cut extra ingredients).

3 Heat a wok or large thick-bottomed frying pan over a high heat. Add the vegetable oil and, when sizzling, add all the vegetables (except the spring onions) and stir-fry until the vegetables are crisp yet tender (a matter of minutes only). Add the soy sauce and lemon juice, Tabasco and sugar, to taste. Add the spring onion segments, toss well, and serve immediately.

Stir-fried Vegetable Shapes with Soy

SERVES 4

6 large spring onions
1 red pepper
1 green pepper
1 medium aubergine
4 medium carrots
150g/6oz button mushrooms
8 tiny new potatoes, parboiled

1 stalk celery, sliced
2 baby turnips, sliced
4 tablespoons salad oil
soy sauce
freshly ground pepper
pinch of crushed dried chillies

1   To prepare vegetables: trim the white bulbs of the spring onions. Cut each in half. Trim the green tops and cut into 0.5cm/¼ inch segments. Cut the peppers in half, remove the seeds, and with a round cutter, stamp one half of each pepper into circles. Cut other halves into arrow shapes, sticks or squares. Cut 0.5cm/¼ inch thick slices down skin sides of aubergine; then with a round cutter cut circles, and cut arrows as above. Peel and slice the carrots 0.5cm/¼ inch thick, and cut the slices into crescent, or moon, shapes. Trim the stalks of the button mushrooms level with the caps, wipe them dry with a damp cloth, and slice into thick slices.

2   Heat the salad oil in a wok (or large frying pan). Sauté the spring onion bulbs for 2 minutes, shaking the pan to ensure they cook evenly. Add the carrot 'moons', new potatotes and sliced turnips and celery, and sauté for 2 more minutes. Add the pepper and aubergine shapes and thickly-sliced mushrooms and continue to cook, shaking pan, until vegetables are crisp tender. Season with soy sauce, freshly ground pepper and crushed dried chillies to taste. Just before serving, add the sliced spring onion tops and warm through.

Curried Vegetables

SERVES 6-8

16 cauliflower florets
16 broccoli florets
4 small courgettes, cut into 2cm/¾
   inch segments
16 small button onions
2 sticks of celery, cut into 2cm/¾
   inch segments

4 medium carrots, peeled and cut into
   2cm/¾ inch segments
salt and freshly ground pepper
juice of ½ a lemon
50g/2oz raisins, plumped in hot water
Madras curry sauce (see p. 221)
crushed dried chillies

1 Cook the first 6 ingredients in boiling salted water with the lemon juice until the vegetables are just tender. Remove from the heat and drain.

2 Meanwhile, make the Madras curry sauce.

3 To serve, add the drained vegetables to the sauce. Stir in the raisins and simmer over a gentle heat until the sauce becomes thick enough just to coat the vegetables. Correct the seasoning, adding a little more curry powder, lemon juice, salt, pepper or crushed dried chillies, to taste. Serve immediately, accompanied by little bowls of the 6 sambals.

Six Sambals for Curried Vegetables

First Dish

1 Wash 4 ripe tomatoes. Skin each tomato by dipping it for 1 minute into boiling water; remove and dip for 1 minute into a bowl filled with iced water and ice cubes. With a sharp knife, remove the skin. Quarter the tomatoes and gently press out the seeds and excess juice. Dice the tomato flesh.

2 In a small bowl, combine the diced tomatoes with 2 tablespoons each finely chopped red onion and green pepper. Add lemon juice and salt and freshly ground pepper, to taste.

Second Dish

1 With the flat blade of a kitchen knife (or chopper), crush 1 finely chopped garlic clove to paste.

2 In a small bowl, mix the garlic paste with 1 tub of Greek yogurt, 1–2 tablespoons finely chopped fresh mint, and lemon juice, salt and freshly ground pepper, to taste.

Third Dish

1 On an ovenproof baking dish, scatter 50g/2oz dried unsweetened coconut and toast in a low oven until golden.

2 In a small bowl, mix the toasted coconut with salt to taste.

Fourth Dish

1 Peel a cucumber and cut it in half lengthwise. With a teaspoon, scoop out the seeds and discard. Dice the cucumber flesh.

2 In a small bowl, combine the diced cucumber with 3 tablespoons chopped spring onion. Season with salt, freshly ground pepper and cayenne pepper to taste. Mix well.

Fifth dish

1 Chop 3 hard-boiled eggs.

2 In a small bowl, combine them with 2 tablespoons each finely chopped red onion and green pepper. Season with lemon juice, salt and cayenne pepper to taste.

Sixth dish

In a small bowl, serve the chutney of your choice: mango, peach or plum, etc.

Vegetable Boiled Dinner with Roasted Garlic Heads

SERVES 4

*4 heads of green (new) garlic, outer
  casings removed*
olive oil
salt and freshly ground pepper
24 baby new potatoes, scrubbed
24 mangetouts, trimmed
225g/8oz baby broad beans
16 baby carrots, scraped

16 asparagus spears, trimmed
16 pea pods (or 100g/4oz shelled peas)

Garnish
*12 cooked quail's or gull's eggs
  (or halved hard-boiled eggs)*
*saffron mayonnaise or green
  mayonnaise*

1 Brush the garlic heads with olive oil. Season with salt and freshly ground pepper and roast in the oven (190°C/375°F/Gas 5) for 12–15 minutes, or until tender.

2 Meanwhile, in a medium saucepan, cook the scrubbed new potatoes in boiling salted water until just tender. With a slotted spoon, transfer the potatoes to a heated serving dish and keep warm. Add the baby carrots to the saucepan and cook for 8-10 minutes, or until carrots are crisp-tender. Transfer them to the heated dish with a slotted spoon. Add the mangetouts, baby broad beans, asparagus spears and pea pods to the saucepan and cook until the vegetables are crisp-tender. Transfer the vegetables to the heated dish and keep warm.

3 Serve on a heated serving dish (or arrange on individual plates), garnish with the boiled eggs, and serve immediately with saffron or green mayonnaise.

Vegetable Marrow Gratin

SERVES 4

900g/2 lb vegetable marrow	salt and freshly ground pepper
1 tablespoon olive oil	pinch or two of crushed dried chillies
2 tablespoon butter	2 tablespoons finely chopped parsley
1 Spanish onion, finely chopped	½ teaspoon dried oregano
1 fat garlic clove, finely chopped	6 tablespoons freshly grated Gruyère cheese
6 canned Italian peeled tomatoes	2 tablespoons freshly grated Parmesan cheese
1 tablespoon tomato purée	4 tablespoons white breadcrumbs

1   Preheat the oven to 190°C/375°F/Gas 5.

2   With a vegetable peeler, peel the vegetable marrow and cut in half. With a sharp spoon, remove the seeds and membranes. Cut the flesh into 2.5cm/1 inch dice.

3   In a large frying pan, heat the olive oil and 1 tablespoon butter, add the finely chopped onion and garlic, and cook over a low heat for 5–7 minutes or until soft and transparent, stirring occasionally with a wooden spoon.

4   Gently press the canned tomatoes to remove the seeds, and chop. Combine with the tomato purée, add to the pan, and cook for a further 2 minutes, stirring constantly. Season with salt, freshly ground pepper and crushed dried chillies to taste.

5   Add the diced marrow, finely chopped parsley and dried oregano, and continue to cook over a moderate heat for 10 minutes or until the marrow begins to tenderize, stirring gently from time to time to mix thoroughly. Transfer to an ovenproof dish.

6   Combine the grated Gruyère and Parmesan and the breadcrumbs, mix well, and sprinkle over the top of the marrow mixture. Dot with remaining butter and bake in the preheated oven for 30 minutes or until the marrow is tender and the topping is crisp, golden and bubbling.

Spicy Garlic & Parsley Mash Fritters with Ackee & Tomato Sauce

SERVES 4–6

450g /1lb potatoes
1.2 litres/2 pints vegetable stock
 (made with stock cubes)
2 garlic cloves, crushed
4–6 spring onions, chopped
crushed dried chillies
2 bunches parsley, finely chopped
chopped chives
salt and freshly ground pepper

dried chick pea flour (gram flour)
chopped cashew nuts
1 can ackee
1 avocado
1 tub of fresh tomato sauce
safflower oil

Garnish
diced avocado

1 Peel the potatoes and cut into large chunks. Cook them in the vegetable stock in a large pan, with the crushed garlic, chopped spring onions, a pinch of crushed dried chillies and chopped parsley.

2 Drain the potatoes, garlic, onion and parsley and mash well. Season with chopped chives, salt and pepper, and leave to cool.

3 When cold, shape the potato mixture into small rectangular (or ball-shaped) fritters. Dip them first in gram flour and then in chopped cashew nuts.

4 In another pan heat the fresh tomato sauce. Drain the juice from the canned ackee and carefully spoon the ackee over the top of the tomato sauce. Put the lid on the pan and simmer gently for 5 minutes, or until the ackee is heated through. Keep warm.

5 In the meantime fry the fritters in a little safflower oil until golden brown, turning them from time to time. With a slotted spoon (or fish slice), transfer the fritters to a heated serving plate.

6 Serve with the ackee and tomato sauce, garnished with chopped avocado.

Vegetable Tempura

SERVES 6

Vegetables

½ medium sized aubergine, sliced
l large sweet potato, peeled and sliced
1 large yellow courgette, cut into rounds
1 red pepper, seeded and cut into thin rings
1 yellow pepper, seeded and cut into thin rings
1 red onion, sliced
2 small fennel bulbs, sliced
2 large parsnips, cut into thin rounds
2 large carrots, scraped and sliced
2 large tomatoes, sliced
6 asparagus spears (tender tops only), cut in
   half lengthwise

Tempura Dipping Sauce

1 vegetable stock cube
300 ml/10 fl oz boiling water
2–4 tablespoons soy sauce
1 slice of fresh ginger, finely chopped
1 tablespoon finely chopped coriander leaves

Tempura Batter

2 eggs
1 tablespoon soy sauce
6 table spoons flour
6 tablespoons cornflour
1 pinch each salt and sugar

1 To make the dipping sauce, combine the vegetable stock cube and boiling water in a small bowl. Stir until the stock cube is completely dissolved. Add the soy sauce and chopped ginger and coriander leaves.

2 To make the batter, combine the eggs, soy sauce and 200ml/8 fl oz cold water in a small bowl and beat (with chopsticks) until the mixture is frothy. In another bowl, combine the flour, cornflour, salt and sugar. Mix well, then lightly stir in the egg and water mixture until the batter is well mixed but still a little lumpy. Do not allow the mixture to stand: for best results, use it immediately. Make more batches of tempura batter as you fry. The batter must be very fresh for best results.

3 Prepare all the vegetables before you are ready to cook and arrange them decoratively in groups on a tray beside your cooking area. In Japan a special tempura pan – a wok with a draining grid attached over the pan at one side – is used to ensure that fat from the tempura-fried foods can drain quickly and easily back into the pan. The food is quickly fried until crisp and golden, and placed immediately on the metal draining grid to drain while the next batch of food is cooked. The food should be fried, drained and eaten as quickly as possible if you want your tempura to be at its crisp best. So, before starting to cook, make sure that you have your tempura batter and dipping sauce ready, and that hot plates are awaiting the hot foods, ready to be served as soon they are cooked. Garnish with canned chick peas, poached mange touts and spring onions.

Round the World Vegetables

Greek Green Beans

SERVES 4

450g/1lb green or runner beans
55g/2¼ oz can tomato purée
4–6 tablespoons olive oil

½ Spanish onion, finely chopped
½ garlic clove, finely chopped
salt and freshly ground pepper

1 Top and tail the green beans and slice them in half lengthways.

2 Mix the tomato purée with 600ml/1 pint water, the olive oil and the finely chopped onion and garlic.

3 Put the bean slices in a saucepan, pour over the tomato mixture, and season with salt and freshly ground pepper to taste. Bring to the boil, lower the heat, and simmer gently, stirring from time to time, for 20 minutes or until the sauce has reduced and the beans are tender.

Note: If fine French beans are used, leave them whole.

Italian Spinach with Pine-nuts and Raisins

SERVES 2–3

butter
finely sliced onion
finely chopped garlic
finely chopped ginger
450g/1lb baby spinach

4 tablespoons raisins, plumped up
  in a little hot water
4 tablespoons pine-nuts
salt and freshly ground pepper

1 Heat 2 tablespoons of butter in a large heavy-based frying pan and sauté the finely chopped onion, garlic and ginger for 1 minute.

2 Add the washed and drained spinach and stir over a medium heat until it wilts.

3 Add the plumped-up raisins and the pine-nuts, browned for a minute in a small dry pan. Stir and cook for 2 minutes. Season with salt and freshly ground pepper to taste. Serve immediately.

(bottom left) Italian Spinach with Pine-nuts and Raisins (see p.151);
(top left) Provençal Potato Bouillabaisse (see p.154);

(right) German Red Cabbage with Orange and Apple (see p.155)

Provençal Potato Bouillabaisse

SERVES 2-3

2 tablespoons finely chopped onion
finely chopped garlic
butter or olive oil
450g/1lb baby new potatoes
900ml/1 ½ pints vegetable stock
  (made with a cube)

2 pinches of saffron
a few basil leaves
salt and freshly ground pepper
2–3 Italian peeled tomatoes
4–6 strips sun-dried tomatoes (in oil)

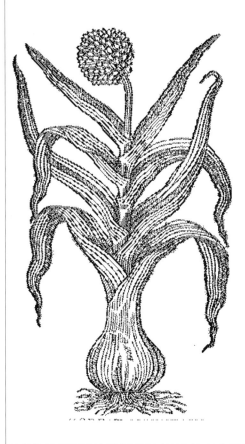

1 Sauté the finely chopped onion and garlic in 2 tablespoons of butter or olive oil in a saucepan until the onions are transparent.

2 Add the peeled and thickly sliced potatoes and cook over a medium heat, stirring for a few minutes.

3 Add the vegetable stock, saffron, basil leaves and salt and freshly ground pepper to taste. Allow stock to simmer over a medium heat for 20 minutes.

4 Towards the end of the cooking time, add a few strips of canned Italian peeled tomatoes and sun-dried tomatoes. Continue to cook until the potatoes are just tender. Serve immediately.

German Red Cabbage with Orange & Apple

SERVES 2–3

2 oranges
2 tart eating apples
butter
4 tablespoons brown sugar
½ red cabbage, thinly sliced
4 tablespoons finely chopped onion

3 tablespoons finely chopped garlic
a little finely chopped ginger
salt and freshly ground pepper
juice of ½–1 lemon
½ bottle red wine
ground nutmeg

1 Grate the rind of 1 orange and reserve for later use. Remove the seeds (and pith) of the orange (and the rind, pith and seeds of the other orange) with a sharp kitchen knife. Then carefully cut the orange flesh into neat wedges, cutting between each fibre segment to release each wedge of orange flesh, working over a bowl to catch excess juices.

2 Peel and core the apples, and cut into thick wedges. Heat 4 tablespoons of butter in a frying pan and sauté the apple and orange segments, turning frequently. Add half the brown sugar and continue to cook until the segments are covered with a pale golden glaze. Remove from the pan and reserve.

3 Place the red cabbage in a large sieve (or colander). Pour over boiling water and allow to drain. Melt more butter in the pan and sauté the finely chopped onion, garlic and ginger. Cook, stirring, until the onion is soft. Add the blanched red cabbage and stir until well covered. Season with salt and freshly ground pepper; add the juice of ½ a lemon (to change the colour of the cabbage to a rich ruby red). Then add the brown sugar, half the red wine and the grated orange rind. Cook for a few minutes, then add a little more wine and continue to cook until the cabbage is tender, but still crisp.

4 When ready to serve, stir in the apple and orange segments together with the liquids they have been cooked in. Correct the seasoning, adding freshly grated nutmeg, a little more lemon juice (if desired) and salt and freshly ground pepper to taste. Serve immediately.

Quick Spanish Beans with Peppers

SERVES 4-6

2–3 cans baked beans
2 yellow peppers
olive oil
½ red onion, finely chopped
1–2 garlic cloves, finely chopped

150ml/¼ pint well-flavoured
*   tomato sauce*
2 tablespoons chopped basil leaves
2 sweet potatoes, cooked and sliced
freshly ground pepper
1–2 pinches crushed dried chillies

1   Pour the canned beans into a large sieve and allow the excess liquids to drain off. Core and seed the peppers; cut 1 pepper into thin rings and dice the other.

2   In a large heatproof casserole, combine 2 tablespoons olive oil with the chopped red onion and garlic and sauté them, stirring constantly, for 3–4 minutes, or until they are transparent. Add the diced yellow pepper and continue to cook, stirring, for 2 more minutes. Then add the tomato sauce and chopped basil leaves and cook for 1 minute more.

3   In the meantime, sauté the pepper rings in olive oil until just tender.

4   When ready to serve, add the drained beans and sweet potatoes to the casserole and heat through. Correct the seasoning, adding freshly ground pepper and crushed dried chillies to taste. Garnish with the sautéed yellow pepper rings and serve immediately.

Italian Sautéed Courgettes

SERVES 4

700g/1 ½lb small courgettes
salt and freshly ground pepper
4 tablespoons flour
4 tablespoons freshly grated
   Parmesan cheese

4 tablespoons olive oil
50g/2 oz butter
1 Spanish onion, coarsely chopped
4 tomatoes skinned, seeded and chopped

1 Poach the courgettes in boiling salted water until just tender, 5–8 minutes. Drain thoroughly, allow to cool and slice thickly. Dry the slices on absorbent paper.

2 Combine the flour and freshly grated Parmesan and season with salt and freshly ground pepper to taste. Toss the courgette slices in this mixture until they are lightly coated.

3 Heat the olive oil in a heavy pan and sauté the courgettes over a moderate heat until they are golden brown on both sides. Remove from the pan with a slotted spoon. Drain thoroughly on absorbent paper and keep hot.

4 Melt the butter in the pan and sauté the coarsely chopped onion until soft and transparent. Add the chopped tomatoes and simmer for 2–3 minutes.

5 Pile the courgettes in the centre of a heated serving dish and surround with the sautéed onion and tomato mixture.

Japanese Grilled Mushrooms

SERVES 6

28 Shiitake mushrooms

Marinade
6 tablespoons peanut oil
2 garlic cloves, finely chopped
1 tablespoon finely chopped fresh ginger

1 bunch of chives, finely chopped
2 tablespoons chopped coriander
1–2 tablespoons light soy sauce
2 tablespoons fresh lime juice
pinch of crushed dried chillies

1   Wash and dry mushrooms. Remove the stalks.

2   In a shallow soup plate, combine the marinade ingredients. Add the mushroom caps, toss well, and allow the mushrooms to take on the marinade flavours for 2 hours.

3   Heat the grill.

4   Thread the mushroom caps horizontally on to each of 6 metal skewers and fill the caps with a little marinade. Place the skewers as near to the heat as possible and grill for 2–4 minutes or until the mushrooms are heated through. Be careful to remove the skewers with a fish slice or wide palette knife to prevent the mushrooms from overturning as you transfer them to individual serving plates.

French Potato & Turnip Gratin

SERVES 6

450g/1lb new potatoes
225g/½lb baby turnips
100g/4oz butter

150ml/5 fl oz double cream
50g/2oz Gruyère cheese, grated
2 tablespoons grated Parmesan cheese
salt and freshly ground pepper

1 Preheat the oven to 170°C/325°F/Gas 3.

2 Peel and slice the potatoes and turnips thinly and soak the slices in cold water for a few minutes. Drain and dry thoroughly with a clean tea-towel.

3 Generously butter a shallow flameproof casserole or deep gratin dish.

4 Place a layer of sliced potatoes and turnips in overlapping rows on the bottom of the dish. Pour over a quarter of the double cream, sprinkle with 2 tablespoons grated cheese (a mixture of Gruyère and Parmesan), dot with butter and season with salt and freshly ground pepper to taste. Continue this process until the dish is full, finishing with a layer of grated cheese.

5 Dot with the butter and cook in the preheated oven for about 1–1¼ hours or until the potatoes are cooked through. If the top becomes too brown, cover with aluminium foil. Serve very hot.

Pasta and Rice

Almond and Raisin Pilaff

SERVES 4

50g/2oz almonds	1 teaspoon cumin
25g/1oz butter	600ml/1 pint vegetable stock
1 medium onion, thinly sliced	salt and freshly ground pepper
225g/8oz long-grain brown rice	crushed dried chillies
1 teaspoon turmeric	50g/2oz raisins

1 Preheat the oven to 180°C/350°F/ Gas 4.

2 Blanch and split the almonds.

3 Melt the butter in a flameproof casserole over a high heat. Add the almonds and stir until they brown evenly. Remove with a slotted spoon.

4 Lower the heat, add the thinly sliced onion and cook until soft. Stir in the rice, turmeric and cumin, and cook for 1½ minutes. Pour in the vegetable stock and bring to the boil. Season with salt, freshly ground pepper and crushed dried chillies to taste. Cover the casserole and cook in the preheated oven for 45 minutes.

5 Stir the almonds and raisins into the casserole, cover, and allow to stand for 10 minutes before serving.

Wild Mushroom Risotto

SERVES 4–6

8–12 dried mushrooms
butter
½ vegetable stock cube, crumbled
½ Spanish onion, finely chopped
350g/12 oz risotto rice
800ml–1 litre/1 ½ –2 pints hot
   vegetable stock

¼–½ teaspoon powdered saffron
salt and freshly ground pepper
crushed dried chillies
6–8 tablespoons freshly grated
   Parmesan cheese

1 Preheat the oven to 180°C/350°F/Gas 4.

2 Soak the dried mushrooms in hot water for several hours. Drain and squeeze dry. Sauté the mushrooms in 2 tablespoons butter with the crumbled vegetable stock cube. Remove from the heat and reserve for later use.

3 Place the finely chopped onion in a deep saucepan with 4 tablespoons butter. Cook slowly for 2–4 minutes, taking care the onion does not become brown. Add the rice and cook over a medium heat, stirring constantly. After a minute or so, stir in 300ml/½ pint hot vegetable stock to which you have added the powdered saffron. Continue cooking, adding stock as necessary and stirring from time to time, until the rice is almost cooked (15 minutes). Season with salt, freshly ground pepper and crushed dried chillies to taste.

4 Cut the reserved mushrooms into small pieces and fold carefully into the risotto. Stir in the freshly grated Parmesan. Place the rice in a well-buttered casserole, cover, and cook in the preheated oven for about 20 minutes.

Aubergine Jambalaya

SERVES 4

2 tablespoons butter
2 tablespoons olive oil
1 Spanish onion, finely chopped
1 green pepper, seeded and
  finely chopped
1 garlic clove, finely chopped
1 large aubergine

150ml/¼ pint dry white wine
900g/28oz can Italian peeled tomatoes
½ teaspoon dried thyme
¼ teaspoon dried basil or oregano
¼ teaspoon Tabasco
salt and freshly ground pepper
225g/8oz risotto rice, boiled until al dente

1 Heat the butter and olive oil in a thick-bottomed casserole and sauté the chopped onion, pepper and garlic until the onion is transparent.

2 Cut the aubergine into 0.5cm/¼ inch thick slices and cut each slice into even-sized fingers. Stir the aubergine fingers into the casserole and sauté for a few minutes longer. Add the dry white wine, tomatoes, dried thyme and basil or oregano, and Tabasco. Season with salt and freshly ground pepper to taste, and bring gently to the boil.

3 Stir in the cooked rice. Reduce the heat, cover the casserole and simmer gently, adding more wine if necessary, for about 10 minutes.

Pilaff Ring with Diced Vegetables

SERVES 4–6

6 large firm tomatoes
150g/6oz button mushrooms
½ Spanish onion, finely chopped
75g/3oz butter
225g/8oz long-grain rice
4 tablespoons dry white wine or cider
800ml/1 ½ pints vegetable stock
   (made with 2 stock cubes)

salt and freshly ground pepper
1 garlic clove, finely chopped
2 tablespoons finely chopped parsley
¼ teaspoon dried oregano
1 avocado pear, peeled and diced
4 spring onions (green parts only), cut
   into 0.5cm/¼ inch segments

1 Preheat the oven to 180°C/350°F/Gas 4.

2 Drop the tomatoes into boiling water and leave for 1 minute. Remove them with a slotted spoon and skin them at once. Remove all the seeds and juice with a teaspoon and dice and reserve the flesh.

3 Slice or quarter the button mushrooms, according to size.

4 Sauté the finely chopped onion in 50g/2oz butter in a medium-sized flameproof casserole until golden. Add the rice and stir over the heat for 1–2 minutes. Pour the dry white wine or cider and the vegetable stock over the rice. Season with salt and freshly ground pepper to taste. Bring to the boil. Cover the casserole and cook in the preheated oven for 14–16 minutes. After about 10 minutes of cooking time, stir once with a fork.

5 Sauté the sliced or quartered button mushrooms in the remaining butter in a large frying pan for 3 minutes. Add the finely chopped garlic and parsley, dried oregano and diced tomato flesh and season with salt and freshly ground pepper to taste. Simmer for 2–3 minutes. Scatter with the diced avocado and keep warm.

6 Form the rice into a ring on a warmed serving plate. Fill the centre with the vegetable mixture and garnish with the spring onion segments.

Spinach Risotto with Red Peppers

SERVES 4

1 Spanish onion, finely chopped
2 garlic cloves, finely chopped
1 red pepper, diced
6 tablespoons olive oil
225g/8oz Arborio rice
1 litre/2 pints hot vegetable stock
450g/1lb spinach

125ml/4 fl oz Marsala
salt and freshly ground pepper
cayenne pepper
1–2 teaspoons Dijon mustard (optional)
6–8 tablespoons freshly grated
  Parmesan cheese

1 In a large thick-bottomed casserole, sauté the finely chopped onion and garlic and the diced pepper in the olive oil until the vegetables are soft and tender.

2 Add the rice to the vegetable mixture and stir over a high heat for 2–3 minutes. Add half the hot vegetable stock and cook over a medium heat, stirring from time to time, until the liquid has been absorbed. Add the remaining stock as necessary.

3 Wash the spinach leaves and trim the stems. Cut the leaves crossways into strips. Just before adding the last of the stock to the rice mixture, add the spinach and Marsala and continue to cook until the liquid has been absorbed and the rice is soft, but firm, and the mixture is creamy.

4 Season generously with salt, freshly ground pepper, cayenne pepper and a little Dijon mustard, if desired. Sprinkle with the freshly grated Parmesan.

Simple Pilaff with Pine-nuts and Shiitake Mushrooms

SERVES 4

butter
1 tablespoon olive oil
100g/4oz Shiitake mushrooms, sliced
225g/8oz long-grain rice
450m/¾ pint light vegetable stock
salt and freshly ground pepper

50g/2oz pine-nuts
squeeze of lemon juice

Garnish
sprigs watercress
freshly grated Parmesan cheese

1 In a heavy, medium saucepan with a tight-fitting lid, heat 1 tablespoon butter and 2 tablespoons olive oil. Add the sliced mushrooms and cook over a medium heat, stirring constantly, until the mushrooms are lightly browned. With a slotted spoon, transfer the mushrooms to a bowl. Reserve.

2 Add the rice to the fats in the pan and stir over a medium heat for 2–3 minutes, or until the grains are transparent and thoroughly coated with hot fat.

3 Add the boiling stock, season with salt and freshly ground pepper, bring to the boil, then reduce the heat to a bare simmer and cover the saucepan tightly with the lid. Leave the rice to simmer for 15–20 minutes, or until the stock has been absorbed, leaving the rice tender but not mushy.

4 When the rice is tender, melt 2 level tablespoons butter in a frying pan. Add the pine-nuts and sauté over a medium heat until golden. Add mushrooms and lemon juice and heat through.

5 To serve, transfer the cooked rice to a heated serving bowl, stir in the nuts and mushrooms, and serve immediately, with freshly grated Parmesan and sprigs of watercress.

Twin Rice Towers with Baby Beets

SERVES 4-6

butter
8 tablespoons finely chopped onion
2 vegetable stock cubes
225g/8oz packet brown and wild rice
225g/8oz packet basmati rice
6 cardamom pods, crushed
12 pink peppercorns (optional)
1–2 pinches of saffron
1 clove, 2 bay leaves
pinch of cayenne or crushed dried chillies

1 lime
1 orange
12 fresh baby beets
2 tablespoons hazelnut oil
1 tablespoon soy sauce
1 tablespoon sugar
1 teaspoon cornflour

Garnish
12 baby bok choy (or baby cos lettuce) leaves

1 To prepare the beets, cut the lime in half, squeeze out the juice into a small bowl and reserve. Do the same with the orange. Reserve. Trim the beets and put them in a pan of water with a little salt and half the squeezed lime peel. Boil gently for 1 hour, or until the beets are tender, adding a little more water from time to time, if necessary.

2 To prepare the brown and wild rice, melt 4 tablespoons butter in a large saucepan, add 4 tablespoons of the chopped onion and cook for a couple of minutes, stirring constantly. Then add a crumbled vegetable stock cube. When the onion is translucent, add the brown and wild rice and stir over a high heat for one minute. Add 800ml/1½ pints water and cook for 1 hour, adding more water during the cooking if necessary. When the rice is cooked through, drain off excess liquid and keep warm.

3 To prepare the basmati rice, melt 4 tablespoons butter in another large saucepan; add 4 tablespoons chopped onion, cook for 1 minute and then crumble in a vegetable stock cube. Stir in the basmati rice. Add the spices and 600ml/1 pint water and leave to simmer until all the water is absorbed and the rice is cooked – about 20 minutes. Remove the clove and bay leaves and keep the rice warm.

4 Drain the cooked beets, and rinse briefly in cold water. Cut off the tops and tails, dip each in iced water and rub off the skins.

5 Into a frying pan pour 2 tablespoons lime juice, 4 tablespoons orange juice, the hazelnut oil, soy sauce, sugar and the cornflour (mixed in 2 tablespoons of water). Stir this mixture over a low heat until the sauce goes transparent. Simmer for 2 minutes.

6 To serve, press any remaining liquid out of the two rice mixtures. Spoon a quantity of each into 2 small moulds or 'towers' (pudding moulds or empty yoghurt pots). Fill the moulds, press down the tops with a spoon, and invert each tower on to a plate. Place 3 or 4 beets by the side of the towers, spoon over some of the sauce, and decorate with the baby bok choy or cos leaves.

Hot Tossed Japanese Noodles & Mushrooms

SERVES 4–6

1 packet dried Chinese mushrooms
2 tablespoons sesame oil
2 tablespoons soy sauce

2 packets Japanese noodles
1 tablespoon vegetable oil
2 tablespoons chopped coriander or parsley

1 Place the dried mushrooms in a small bowl and add 800 ml/1½ pints boiling water to cover. Let the mushrooms steep in water until soft. Remove from bowl and squeeze dry. Add 1 tablespoon each of sesame oil and soy sauce and mix well.

2 Bring 1.25 litres/2½ pints water to the boil. Add the Japanese noodles together with the contents of the small seasoning packets (found in each packet of noodles). Stir until the noodles are separated, cooking for 2 minutes in all.

3 Drain the noodles and transfer to a large bowl. Add the marinated mushrooms and the remaining sesame oil, soy sauce and vegetable oil. Stir well.

4 Transfer to an hors d'œuvre dish and sprinkle with chopped coriander or parsley.

Pasta with Green Vegetables and Red Peppers

SERVES 4

450g/1lb fresh tagliarini or tagliolini
  (thin-cut noodles)
4 tablespoons butter
salt and freshly ground pepper
crushed dried chillies
freshly grated Parmesan cheese, or thin
  curls of Parmesan
1 red pepper, cut into thin strips

225g/8oz very fine French beans
8 asparagus spears
225g/8oz mangetouts
¼ vegetable stock cube
1–2 courgettes, according to size
100g/4oz frozen peas, defrosted
4 tablespoons butter
salt and freshly ground pepper

1 Trim the French beans and cut each bean into 2 even-sized segments. Trim the mangetouts. Cut each asparagus spear into 2 or 3 even-sized segments (using only the tender parts). Slice the courgettes into thin slices.

2 In a large frying pan, bring to the boil the butter and enough water to cover the vegetables. Add the red pepper strips, French beans, asparagus and mangetouts to the pan, then add ¼ vegetable stock cube and allow the vegetables to cook for 4 minutes. Add the thinly sliced courgettes and the peas and continue to cook for 1 or 2 minutes more. The vegetables should be crisp-tender. Drain the vegetables over a small bowl to reserve the juices.

3 Meanwhile cook the pasta in a large pot of boiling salted water for 5 minutes, or until tender but still *al dente*. Drain.

4 When ready to serve, return the pasta to the pan. Add the butter and a little of the reserved juices from the vegetables to moisten. Season to taste with salt, freshly ground pepper and a pinch of crushed dried chillies and toss until the strands are hot and evenly coated. Transfer to a heated serving dish, garnish with the cooked vegetables and serve immediately, with the Parmesan.

Tagliolini with Sun-dried Tomatoes, Courgettes and Yellow Peppers

SERVES 4

450g/1lb tagliolini (thin-cut noodles)
2 tablespoons olive oil
1 stick of lemon grass, finely chopped
5cm/2 inch piece fresh ginger, peeled
  and finely chopped
4 garlic cloves, finely chopped
½ a vegetable stock cube, crumbled
4 sun-dried tomatoes, cut into thin strips
2 courgettes (dark green outside parts
  only) cut into thin strips

1 yellow pepper, cut into thin strips
salt and freshly ground pepper
pinch of crushed dried chillies
juice of ½ lemon

Garnish
tiny sprigs (or single large leaves) of
  fresh coriander

1   Cook the pasta in a large pot of boiling salted water until just tender, (4–7 minutes for fresh tagliolini , 11 minutes for dried). In the meantime, make the sauce. In a large heat-proof frying pan, heat the olive oil. Add the finely chopped lemon grass, ginger and garlic, and cook over a medium heat, stirring constantly, until transparent. Stir in the crumbled vegetable stock cube.

2   Add the strips of sun-dried tomato, courgette and yellow pepper and cook, stirring until the vegetables are soft, but still crisp. Add salt, freshly ground pepper and crushed dried chillies to taste. Add the lemon juice and remove from the heat.

3   In another, larger frying pan, heat the pasta in 2 tablespoons olive oil. Add salt, freshly ground pepper and crushed dried chillies, to taste. Add the stir-fried vegetables and seasonings, toss well, and transfer to a heated serving dish, piling the pasta high on the dish. Serve immediately.

Three-Coloured Pasta

SERVES 4

6 tablespoons olive oil
1½ teaspoons Madras curry powder
1 pinch crushed dried chillies
4 tablespoons butter
1 vegetable stock cube, crumbled
3–4 carrots, cut into julienne strips
   like pasta
3–4 courgettes, cut into julienne strips
   like pasta

350g/12 oz tagliarini or linguine
salt and freshly ground pepper
8 spring onions (green parts only),
   cut into quarters lengthwise
1 large egg yolk
150ml/¼ pint crème fraîche
tiny sprigs fresh coriander
freshly grated Parmesan cheese

1 Combine the olive oil, curry powder and crushed dried chillies in a small jar, cover tightly, shake well, and set aside to allow the flavours to fuse.

2 In a large frying pan, combine 2 tablespoons butter with the crumbled vegetable stock cube. Add the julienne strips of carrot and courgette and just enough water to cover them. Bring gently to the boil. Lower the heat and simmer, stirring occasionally, for 2–4 minutes, or until the vegetables are just tender. Drain.

3 Cook the tagliarini in a large pan of boiling salted water until just tender. Drain and return to the pan. Shake the curried oil and pour it over the pasta. Season with salt and freshly ground pepper, to taste.

4 Add the julienned vegetables, the spring onion strips and the remaining butter to the pan. Stir the egg yolk into the *crème fraîche* and add this to the pan too. Shake the pan over a moderate heat until the pasta and vegetables are heated through and lightly coated with the curried cream.

5 Correct the seasoning – adding a little more salt, pepper or crushed dried chillies. Garnish with coriander and serve immediately, accompanied by a bowl of freshly grated Parmesan.

Farfalle with Summer Tomato Sauce

SERVES 4

6 medium-sized tomatoes or Italian
  canned peeled tomatoes
150ml/ ¼ pint olive oil
12–18 basil leaves, cut into thin strips
1–2 teaspoons lemon juice

pinch of dried oregano
salt and freshly ground pepper
freshly grated Parmesan cheese
450g/1lb farfalle (bowknots)
12 black olives

1 If using fresh tomatoes, peel, seed and either coarsely chop them or cut them into strips, being careful not to lose the juices. If using canned tomatoes, drain, press out the seeds and cut the flesh into strips.

2 Combine the tomatoes, olive oil, basil strips and lemon juice to taste. Season with dried oregano, salt and freshly ground pepper to taste, and toss. Stir in a few table-spoons of freshly grated Parmesan. Reserve cold sauce.

3 Cook the farfalle in 3–4 litres/6–8 pints boiling salted water for 12 minutes or until *al dente*. Drain and transfer to a heated serving dish. Add the cold sauce, garnish with the black olives and serve with freshly grated Parmesan.

Tortiglioni with Vodka and Lemon

SERVES 3-4

2 lemons
6 tablespoons butter
2–3 tablespoons vodka
1–2 tablespoons tomato ketchup
salt and freshly ground pepper

pinch or two of crushed dried chillies
350g/12oz tortiglioni or penne
(or other shaped pasta)
50g/2oz coarsely grated walnuts
freshly grated Parmesan cheese

1 Scrub the lemons with a brush; rinse under running water and dry thoroughly. Then, with a sharp knife, cut the peel of the lemons into long thin strips. Cut the strips crosswise into thin matchsticks.

2 Melt the butter in a pan, add lemon matchsticks and cook over a medium heat for 3 minutes. Do not allow the butter to colour. Stir in the vodka and just enough tomato ketchup to lightly colour the sauce, season with salt, freshly ground pepper and dried crushed chillies to taste, and remove the pan from the heat.

3 Bring a large saucepan of salted water to the boil; add the pasta and cook for 11 minutes or until the pasta is *al dente*, just tender but not overcooked.

4 To serve, transfer the drained pasta to a large frying pan, add the lemon and vodka sauce and the coarsely grated nuts, and toss over a high heat until the pasta is warmed through. Correct the seasoning and serve immediately, accompanied by a bowl of freshly grated Parmesan.

Farfalle with Summer Tomato Sauce (see p.174)

Tortiglioni with Vodka and Lemon (see p.175)

Pasta Bows & Bells with Kasha & Chestnuts

SERVES 4–6

225g/8oz pasta bows
225g/8oz pasta bells (campanelli)
100g/4oz kasha (buckwheat groats)
600ml/1 pint vegetable stock
 (made with a cube)
1 can peeled chestnuts
4 tablespoons butter
1 tablespoon finely chopped ginger
2 pinches of paprika
2 pinches of cinnamon

pinch of crushed dried chillies
salt and freshly ground pepper
soy sauce

Garnish
2–3 Italian peeled tomatoes, seeded
 and cut into thin strips
spring onions (green part only),
 cut into thin strips
freshly grated Parmesan cheese

1   Cook the pasta shapes in boiling water until tender, and drain over a bowl.

2   Roast the buckwheat groats in a dry frying pan over medium heat for 5 minutes, stirring constantly, until they are lightly browned. Add 450ml/¼ pint vegetable stock and simmer for about 10 minutes or until the buckwheat is tender and the liquid reduced to a few tablespoons.

3   In another pan sauté the chestnuts in 2 tablespoons of the butter. Season with chopped ginger, 2 pinches each of paprika and cinnamon and a pinch of crushed dried chillies. Add 4–6 tablespoons of vegetable stock and soy sauce to taste, and stir until well mixed. Cook for a while on high heat to reduce the liquids and make a sauce. Stir in the buckwheat mixture and keep warm.

4   Clean the frying pan and melt the remaining butter. Add the cooked pasta and toss in the butter to heat through. Season with salt and freshly ground black pepper to taste.

5   To serve, arrange pasta on a heated serving dish. Spoon over the kasha and chestnut mixture; garnish with strips of tomato and spring onion and freshly grated Parmesan.

Desserts

Green Fruit Posset

SERVES 4–6

4–6 kiwi fruits, according to size
finely grated zest and juice of 2 lemons
600ml/1 pint double cream
150ml/5 fl oz white wine
1 tablespoon sugar
3 medium-sized egg whites

Decoration
candied violets (or fresh raspberries
    or strawberries)
slices of kiwi fruit, cut in half

1 Peel the kiwi fruit and cut 4–6 slices to reserve as decoration. Cut the remainder into chunks and process in a food processor with the lemon juice until smooth.

2 In a large clean bowl, combine the finely grated lemon zest and double cream and whisk until peaks form. Stir in the dry white wine and sugar and then whisk in the kiwi mixture little by little.

3 In another bowl, and using a clean whisk, whisk the egg whites until they form stiff peaks and fold them into the kiwi/cream mixture. Chill.

4 Just before serving, whisk the posset one more time (it will have separated in the refrigerator) and pile into a glass serving dish. Decorate with candied violets and halved kiwi slices, or, when in season, fresh raspberries or strawberries.

Poached Peaches and Pears in Burgundy (see p.182)

Poached Peaches & Pears in Burgundy

SERVES 6

450ml/¾ pint red burgundy
3 segments each of thinly pared
 peel of lemon and orange
1 vanilla pod
2 tablespoons peppercorns

5 tablespoons liquid honey
6 bay leaves
1 cinnamon stick
6 large yellow peaches
6 large ripe dessert pears

1   In a large saucepan, combine the burgundy, citrus peel, vanilla pod and peppercorns (tied up in a muslin bag) and bring gently to the boil. Skim and stir the honey into the hot liquid. Remove the saucepan from the heat; add the bay leaves and the cinnamon and allow the flavours to amalgamate while you prepare the fruits.

2   In another saucepan, bring 2 pints water to the boil. Place the peaches in the boiling water and bring the water to the boil again. Cook the peaches for a few minutes over a moderate heat, then remove from the water and gently remove the skins from the peaches. Peel the pears, being careful to remove as little of their flesh as possible.

3   Put the peaches in the hot spiced burgundy liquid. Bring to the boil again and cook for 10 minutes, or until the peaches test tender with the point of a skewer. Remove the peaches from the pan with a slotted spoon and place in a shallow bowl to cool.

4   Place the peeled pears in the hot liquid; bring to the boil again and boil for 10 minutes, or until the pears test tender with the point of a skewer. Remove the pears from the pan with a slotted spoon and place them in a shallow bowl to cool. Refrigerate the peaches and pears until ready to serve.

5   Meanwhile, remove the spices from the burgundy syrup and reserve. Over a high heat, reduce the syrup to the desired consistency. Remove the pan from the heat and allow the syrup to cool to room temperature. Place in the refrigerator with the fruit.

6   To serve, decorate each pear with a bay leaf. Cut the cinnamon stick into 6 equal segments and decorate each peach with a piece of cinnamon. Sprinkle a few peppercorns over the fruit. Pour a little syrup over the peaches and pears and serve the remainder of the syrup separately.

Apricot Bavarois

SERVES 6

1 tablespoon cornflour
600ml/1 pint milk
6 large egg yolks
225g/8oz caster sugar
900g/28oz canned apricot halves in syrup
15g/½oz gelatine (see note, p.187)

juice of 2 lemons
4 tablespoons very cold milk
300ml/10 fl oz double cream
melted butter
fresh fruits in season
whipped cream

1 Bring some water to the boil in the bottom of a double saucepan then reduce the heat so the water is lightly simmering. Mix the cornflour in a bowl with 4 tablespoons milk. Pour the remaining milk into the top pan and scald over a gentle, direct heat. Pour the milk on to the cornflour mixture, stirring, and return to the pan. Bring the milk to the boil over a medium heat, stirring continuously, and simmer for 2–3 minutes. Leave to cool for 5–10 minutes, stirring to prevent a skin forming.

2 In a large bowl, whisk the egg yolks with the caster sugar until pale and so thick that the mixture falling from the lifted beaters will leave a trail on the rest of the mixture. Gradually whisk in the thickened milk. Return the mixture to the top pan and cook over the simmering water, stirring constantly with a wooden spoon, until the custard is thick enough to coat the back of the spoon. Remove the pan from the heat and plunge the base into cold water. Continue stirring for 1–2 minutes until custard has cooled slightly.

3 Drain the apricot halves and pour 150ml/5 fl oz syrup into a small bowl. Sprinkle the gelatine on to the syrup and leave to soften for a few minutes. Put the bowl in a saucepan of hot water and stir until the gelatine has completely dissolved.

4 Turn the custard into a large bowl and pour in the dissolved gelatine in a thin stream, stirring continuously. Reserve enough apricot halves to decorate the base of a 1.5 litre/3 pint decorative mould. Cut each remaining half into 6 slices and stir into the custard with the lemon juice. Chill until on the point of setting.

5 Add the cold milk to the double cream and whisk until thick, but not stiff. Fold the whipped cream into the almost set custard.

6 Brush inside of mould with melted butter and arrange reserved apricot halves over base. Pour in the cold, but not set, custard cream, cover and chill for 2 hours or until firm.

7 Unmould the bavarois on to a flat serving plate. Decorate with fresh fruits and cream.

Moroccan Fruit Tarts

SERVES 4

Pastry
6 sheets filo pastry
4 tablespoons melted butter
icing sugar

Almond Filling
6 tablespoons ground toasted almonds
4 tablespoons caster sugar
½–1 teaspoon ground cinnamon

Fruit Topping and Glaze
1 mango
50g/2oz blueberries
50g/2 oz redcurrants
1 tablespoon lemon juice
1 tablespoon Kirsch
1–2 tablespoons caster sugar

1 Place the sheets of filo pastry on a flat work surface. With a sharp knife, cut out 12 17cm/7 inch squares. Cover with a damp towel until ready for use.

2 Brush 4 7cm/3 inch ramekins with melted butter and line each with l filo square.

3 In a small bowl, combine the toasted almonds, caster sugar and cinnamon. Sprinkle l teaspoon of the almond mixture into the bottom of each pastry-lined ramekin and cover with another sheet of filo pastry, turning the sheet around one quarter turn to create a 'flower' effect. (see picture). Sprinkle each pastry-lined ramekin with almond mixture, as above, and repeat with a third sheet of pastry (turning the sheet around one quarter, as above). Sprinkle with the remaining almond mixture. (N.B. I find it useful to use marble-sized crumpled-up balls of aluminium foil to hold up the points of the pastry (to keep pastry leaves free-standing) while baking.

4 Preheat the oven to 190°C/375°F/Gas 5. Bake the tarts in the preheated oven for 5 minutes, or until the pastry is crisp and golden. Remove the tarts from the ramekins and allow to cool on pastry racks. Just before serving, sprinkle with a little icing sugar.

5 To make the glazed fruits, peel the mango over a bowl, to catch the juices and cut carefully into slices with a sharp knife. Wash and hull the blueberries and redcurrants. To make the glaze, combine mango juices with lemon juice, Kirsch and caster sugar to taste in a small saucepan. Over a gentle heat, stirring constantly, cook until the sugar has melted.

6 To assemble the tarts, arrange the mango slices in each pastry case, top with blueberries and redcurrants and spoon over a little of the fruit glaze. Serve at once.

Tulipe Glacée

SERVES 8

125g/5oz flour	*1 fresh pineapple, peeled, cored*
125g/5oz sugar	*and diced*
2 egg yolks	*Kirsch*
3 egg whites	*vanilla ice-cream*
1 large orange, buttered (see method)	*whipped cream*

1 Preheat the oven to 180°C/350°F/Gas 4.

2 Sift the flour and icing sugar into a mixing bowl. Add the egg yolks and whites and mix well.

3 Butter a cold baking sheet and mark 4 circles on it with a 16cm/6¼ inch – 19cm/ 7½ inch saucer. Spread 1 dessertspoon of the mixture over each circle, using the back of a teaspoon. Bake in the preheated oven for 5–6 minutes or until just turning brown at the edges.

4 Remove each round from the baking sheet, turn over, and working quickly, place each circle over the top of the buttered orange. Place a tea-towel over the pastry to prevent burning your hands, and mould the pastry to fit the orange. Remove, and continue as above, baking 2–4 circles each time and shaping them over the orange as you go. The cases will keep for days in a biscuit tin. This recipe makes 12–16 tulipes.

5 Just before serving, fill 8 cases with diced fresh pineapple which you have marinated in Kirsch, add a scoop of vanilla ice-cream, and decorate with whipped cream.

Cold Chocolate Soufflé

SERVES 8

25g/1oz gelatine or substitute*
4 egg yolks
100g/4oz caster sugar
75g/3oz semi-sweet chocolate, melted
600ml/1 pint milk
300ml/½ pint double cream, whipped
4 egg whites, stiffly beaten

Decoration
grated chocolate
whipped cream
chocolate batons

1 Tie a band of double greaseproof paper around the outside of a 15–17cm/6–7 inch soufflé dish to stand 7cm/3 inches above the rim of the dish (or use 4 individual soufflé dishes).

2 Soak the gelatine in a little cold water until soft.

3 Combine the egg yolks, caster sugar and melted chocolate.

4 Heat the milk to boiling point and whisk into the chocolate mixture until well blended. Pour the mixture into the top of a double saucepan and cook over simmering water, stirring constantly, until the mixture coats the back of a spoon. Strain, if necessary. Add the gelatine and allow to cool. Stir over iced water until the mixture begins to set.

5 Fold the whipped double cream into the chocolate mixture, then the stiffly beaten egg whites. Pour into the prepared soufflé dish or dishes, chill until set.

6 Remove the band of paper. Coat the sides of the soufflé with grated chocolate and decorate the top with piped whipped cream and chocolate batons.

* Substitutes for gelatine include agar agar and Gelozone. Follow directions on packaging for quantities and method of use.

(left) Cold Chocolate Soufflé (see p.187);
(centre) Chocolate Cake with Jamaican Rum Sauce (see p.190);

(top right) Green Fruit Bowl (see p.191)

Chocolate Cake with Jamaican Rum Sauce

SERVES 4

20cm/8 inch square chocolate cake slice
  (2.5cm/1 inch thick), trimmed and
  cut into 4 portions

Jamaican Rum Sauce
350ml 12 fl oz carton coffee ice-cream,
  softened to whipped cream consistency
4–6 tablespoons chopped praline
2–4 tablespoons Jamaican rum, or
  crème de cacao

Garnish
1 orange, peeled and cut into segments
1 orange, unpeeled, cut into thin half slices
4 thin slices crystallized ginger, cut
  into matchsticks
grated chocolate

1 To make the Jamaican rum sauce, combine the softened coffee ice-cream, chopped praline and Jamaican rum (or crème de cacao) and place in the freezer for 10 minutes to firm up a little.

2 Place 1 portion of chocolate cake on each of 4 individual dessert plates. Decorate each cake slice with orange segments, unpeeled halved orange slices and sticks of preserved ginger.

3 Spoon a little chilled sauce on to each plate. Sprinkle with grated chocolate and serve the remaining sauce separately.

Green Fruit Bowl

SERVES 4

2 bananas
2 limes
4 kiwi fruit, peeled and thinly sliced
1 bunch of seedless white grapes
½ a honeydew melon
6 tablespoons ginger syrup

Garnish
crème fraîche
sprigs of mint

1 Peel and slice the bananas and pour over the juice of 1 lime. Allow to stand for a few minutes to absorb the flavours. Drain, reserving the marinade.

2 Slice the remaining lime in half lengthways and cut each half into the thinnest slices possible. Cut balls from the melon with a melon baller.

3 Combine the thinly sliced kiwi fruit with the white grapes, banana and lime slices and melon balls in a glass serving bowl. Pour over the ginger syrup and marinade, and toss lightly. To serve, fill individual glasses with the green fruit salad and garnish each glass with a dollop of *crème fraîche* and 1 tiny sprig of fresh mint.

Chilled Fruits with Chocolate Fondue

SERVES 4

225g/8oz good-quality dark plain chocolate, broken into pieces
150ml/5 fl oz double cream
1–2 tablespoons brandy
1 large mango, peeled and cut into slices
l large papaya, peeled, seeds removed and cut into slices
225g/8oz strawberries
175g/6 oz green seedless grapes
225g/8 oz physalis (Chinese gooseberries), with their paper lantern, peeled back
1 star fruit, sliced

1 Arrange sliced mango, papaya, strawberries, grapes, physalis and star fruit on a large serving dish. Brush surfaces of cut fruit with lemon juice. Cover the dish with clingfilm and chill.

2 To make the fondue, put the chocolate and cream into a fondue pot or small saucepan and heat gently until the chocolate has melted. Stir in the brandy and beat until smooth. Keep the pot warm over a fondue burner or keep gently heating.

3 To serve, remove the clingfilm from the dish of fruit and serve the cold fruit platter and hot chocolate sauce. Guests help themseves, dipping the fruit into the hot sauce.

Oranges in Burgundy Syrup

SERVES 4

225g/8 oz sugar
170ml/6 fl oz red burgundy
1 clove
1 cinnamon stick, broken in half

2 strips of lemon peel
2 strips of orange peel
4 large oranges
slivers of orange peel

1 Combine the sugar and 150ml/¼ pint water in a thick-bottomed saucepan and bring to the boil.

2 Add 150ml/¼ pint red burgundy and the clove, broken cinnamon stick and strips of lemon and orange peel to the pan. Bring to the boil again and continue to cook until reduced to a syrup. Add the remaining red Burgundy.

3 Peel the oranges and cut away all the white pith with a sharp knife. Slip the knife blade between each segment and membrane and cut the segment out. Remove any pips.

4 Arrange the orange segments in a glass serving bowl and pour over the hot syrup. Allow to cool. Chill.

5 Just before serving, decorate the bowl with slivers of orange peel.

Watermelon with Strawberry Cream

SERVES 4

1–2 watermelon slices, 2.5cm/1 inch thick, chilled
300ml/½ pint double cream, chilled

450g/1lb strawberries, hulled and chilled
1 tablespoon Kirsch
sugar

1 Peel the chilled watermelon slices and cut the flesh into 2.5cm/1 inch cubes. Arrange in 4 individual bowls.

2 Whip the chilled double cream.

3 Reserve 4–8 strawberries for decoration and place the remainder in the bowl of an electric blender or food processor. Blend until smooth. Add to the whipped cream and flavour with Kirsch and sugar to taste.

4 Spoon the strawberry cream over the watermelon cubes and decorate with the reserved strawberries.

Oriental Fruit Salad

SERVES 4

1 ripe melon, chilled
75g/3 oz canned kumquats
75g/3 oz canned mandarin orange segments
4 tablespoons dry sherry, dry white wine or lemon juice

1 Remove the top of the chilled melon by tracing 'V'-shaped incisions round the fruit and cutting through each incision to the centre so that the top can be lifted off in one piece.

2 Using a melon baller, scoop out the flesh from the top and two-thirds from the base.

3 Combine the melon balls with the kumquats and mandarin orange segments. Flavour with the dry sherry, dry white wine or lemon juice, and arrange the fruit in the melon shell.

Pears Belle Hélène

SERVES 6

6 firm ripe dessert pears
150g/6oz sugar
thinly pared strips of lemon peel
vanilla essence
450–600ml/¾–1 pint vanilla ice-cream

Chocolate sauce
150g/6oz bitter chocolate
50g/2oz butter
6 tablespoons crème fraîche
6 tablespoons single cream
2 tablespoons rum or brandy
vanilla essence (optional)
shavings of chocolate

1   Preheat the oven to 180°C/350°F/Gas 4. Peel, halve and core the pears, and arrange them in one layer in a large baking dish, flat side down.

2   Combine the sugar and lemon peel with 450ml/¼ pint water in a heavy pan. Bring to the boil, stirring, until the sugar has melted. Flavour to taste with vanilla essence.

3   Pour the syrup over the pears; cover the dish tightly with foil and bake for 15–20 minutes, or until the pears are tender but not disintegrating. With a slotted spoon or fish slice, transfer pears carefully to a large, shallow dish.

4   Pour the syrup into a pan and boil until reduced to a quarter of the original volume, then strain over the pears. Cool, then chill until ready to serve.

5   Meanwhile, make the chocolate sauce. Stir the chocolate and the butter over hot water until smoothly blended. Gradually beat in the *crème fraîche* and single cream, then bring to the boil and simmer over direct heat for 2–5 minutes, stirring constantly. Flavour to taste with rum or brandy and a few drops of vanilla essence, if desired. Serve with vanilla ice-cream, and decorate with shavings of chocolate.

Petits Pots au Chocolat à l'Orange

SERVES 6

450g/1lb dark bitter chocolate

4 oranges

50g/2 oz butter

4–6 tablespoons Grand Marnier or Cognac

4 egg yolks

2 egg whites

1 Break the chocolate into the top of a double saucepan. Finely grate the rind of 1 orange and add it to the chocolate. Squeeze the juice of the grated orange plus 2 more oranges (keeping the last one for garnish), and add the juice to the chocolate mixture, together with the butter. Heat over simmering water, stirring occasionally, until the chocolate has melted. Remove from the heat, add 2 tablespoons Grand Marnier or Cognac, and beat thoroughly until smooth.

2 Beat the egg yolks thoroughly in a bowl. Strain in the chocolate mixture through a fine sieve, beating constantly. Cool.

3 In another bowl, beat the egg whites until stiff but not dry. Fold into the chocolate mixture gently but thoroughly with a spatula.

4 Divide the mixture equally between individual soufflé pots and chill until set. (Do not use metal pots, as the chocolate may discolour.)

5 Just before serving, cut thin slices from the centre of the remaining orange. Quarter each slice and lay 2 quarters, point to point, on top of each pot. Pour over a teaspoonful of Grand Marnier or Cognac and swirl the pot around very gently so that the entire surface is moistened. Serve immediately.

Pineapple and Orange Ice-Cream

SERVES 4

4 large oranges
4 pineapple slices, peeled and cored
4 scoops of vanilla ice-cream

chilled whipped cream
chocolate vermicelli
toasted slivered almonds

1   Peel the oranges with a sharp knife and cut away all the white pith. Slip the knife blade between each segment and the membrane and cut the segment out. Remove pips.

2   Place 1 pineapple slice on to each of 4 individual serving plates. Arrange the orange segments in flower shapes on each plate. Place 1 scoop of vanilla ice-cream in the hollow of each pineapple slice. Top with chilled whipped cream and scatter over chocolate vermicelli and toasted slivered almonds.

Vanilla Ice-Cream with Brandied Mincemeat

SERVES 4

400g/14oz jar mincemeat
50g/2 oz butter
4 tablespoons Cognac

4 large or 8 small scoops of vanilla ice-cream
2 orange slices, halved

1   Combine the mincemeat, butter and Cognac in a thick-bottomed saucepan and cook, stirring constantly, until the sauce is hot and bubbling.

2   Place 1 large or 2 small scoops of vanilla ice-cream in each of 4 chilled parfait glasses or ice-cream coupes. Top with brandied mincemeat and decorate each with 1 half slice of orange.

Spanish Banana Dessert

SERVES 4

5 large bananas
lemon juice
50g/2oz butter
125ml/4fl oz dry sherry

demerara sugar
300ml/½ pint double cream, chilled
½ teaspoon vanilla essence
100g/4 oz jar maraschino cherries

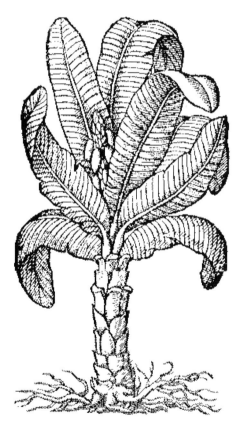

1 Peel 4 bananas, cut in half lengthways, and brush with lemon juice to prevent the flesh turning brown. Peel the remaining banana, cut into thin slices and brush with lemon juice.

2 Melt 15g/½oz butter in each of 4 individual flameproof serving dishes large enough to take the banana halves side by side, and sauté the bananas until golden brown on each side. Remove from the heat, pour 2 tablespoons dry sherry into each dish and sprinkle with demerara sugar.

3 Whip the chilled double cream until soft peaks form, and fold in the vanilla essence.

4 Decorate each dish with swirls of the vanilla-flavoured cream and maraschino cherries, and sprinkle with demerara sugar.

Banana Rum Crunch

SERVES 4–6

225g/8 oz digestive biscuits, crushed
3 tablespoons caster sugar
4 tablespoons melted butter
150ml/¼ pint double cream, whipped
1 banana, peeled, sliced and sprinkled
   with lemon juice
black treacle

Filling
3 bananas
2 tablespoons caster sugar
2 tablespoons Jamaican rum
150ml/¼ pint double cream, whipped

1 Preheat the oven to 190°C/375°F/Gas 5.

2 Combine the crushed digestive biscuits, caster sugar and melted butter.

3 Press the biscuit crumb mixture firmly and evenly into an 18x18x2.5cm/7½x7½x1 inch ovenproof glass dish. Bake in the preheated oven for 15 minutes. Allow to cool.

4 To make the filling, peel and chop the bananas and combine with the caster sugar and Jamaican rum, mashing to a smooth pulp. Fold into the whipped cream.

5 Pour the filling into the biscuit crust. Pipe the whipped cream around the edge of the filling and top with the banana slices. Decorate with a thin dribble of black treacle trickled from the point of a teaspoon.

Brandy Apple Fritters

SERVES 4

3 medium-sized cooking apples
2 tablespoons sugar
4–6 tablespoons brandy
100g/4oz flour
¼ teaspoon salt
1 egg, beaten

1 tablespoon melted butter
150ml/¼ pint light ale
oil
caster sugar
double cream

1 Peel and core the apples and cut each one into 4 thick rings. Sprinkle with the sugar and brandy. Reserve.

2 Sift together the flour and salt. Add the beaten egg, melted butter and half the light ale, and beat until smooth. Gradually beat in the remaining ale. Reserve batter until ready to use.

3 Preheat the grill to high.

4 Heat the oil in a deep-fat frier to 180°C/350°F, or until a cube of stale bread dropped into the oil turns brown in 60 seconds.

5 Dip the brandied apple slices in the batter, draining carefully, and deep-fry in the preheated oil for 3 minutes or until crisp and golden brown. Drain on absorbent paper. Transfer to a heated serving platter, cover with a thick layer of caster sugar, and grill under the preheated grill until the sugar begins to caramelize. Serve with a jug of double cream.

Amaretto Stuffed Crêpes

SERVES 4

2 tablespoons caster sugar
2 tablespoons Amaretto liqueur
300ml/½ pint double cream, whipped
8 cooked sweet crêpes
crumbled Amaretti biscuits

Apricot Sauce
200ml/8 fl oz apricot jam
4 tablespoons Amaretto liqueur

1 Fold the caster sugar and 2 tablespoons Amaretto liqueur into the whipped cream.

2 Divide the Amaretto-flavoured cream between the crêpes and roll them up.

3 To make the apricot sauce, combine the apricot jam, 4 tablespoons Amaretto liqueur and 4 tablespoons water in a thick-bottomed saucepan and heat through. Pass the sauce through a fine sieve.

4 Place 2 crêpes on each of 4 individual serving plates. Sprinkle each crêpe generously with crumbled Amaretti biscuits and spoon the apricot sauce around the crêpes.

Amaretto Mousses in Orange Shells

SERVES 6

6 large oranges
6 medium egg yolks
6 tablespoons caster sugar
6 tablespoons Amaretto liqueur
200ml/8 fl oz double cream, whipped

Decoration
125ml/4 fl oz double cream, whipped
6 Amaretti biscuits, crushed
sprigs of fresh mint
fresh raspberries

1 Using a sharp knife, slice off the top of each orange. Using a grapefruit knife and a small metal spoon, carefully scoop out all the orange pulp and enough of the pith to leave a firm shell. Place the orange shells on a small baking sheet or a small metal tin. Arrange them closely together so they support each other and do not topple over. Set aside.

2 Combine the egg yolks, caster sugar and Amaretto liqueur in a mixing bowl and beat until smooth and creamy. Using a large metal spoon, fold in the whipped cream (the mixture will be fairly liquid).

3 Fill the orange shells with the egg yolk and cream mixture. Place in the freezing compartment of the refrigerator and leave for at least 8 hours or overnight until the mixture is firm.

4 Twenty minutes before serving, transfer the oranges to the refrigerator to soften a little.

5 Just before serving, decorate the tops with piped whipped cream and crushed Amaretti biscuits. Spike each orange with a sprig of fresh mint and decorate the plate with fresh raspberries.

Pears in Gorgonzola

SERVES 4

4 large pears
lemon juice
25g/1oz pistachio nuts or walnuts,
  coarsely chopped
paprika
celery leaves
sprigs of mint or watercress

Filling
50g/2oz softened butter
100g/4oz Gorgonzola cheese
1 tablespoon Cognac
freshly ground pepper
15g/½oz pistachio nuts or walnuts,
  coarsely chopped

1 Peel the pears, halve them lengthways, and core them, leaving the stems intact. Brush them with lemon juice to prevent the flesh turning brown.

2 To make the filling, cream together the softened butter, Gorgonzola and Cognac and season with freshly ground pepper to taste. Add the coarsely chopped pistachio nuts or walnuts.

3 Insert a star nozzle into a piping bag and fill the bag with filling. Pipe the filling into the cavities of the pear halves and sandwich them together.

4 Stand 1 pear upright on each of 4 individual serving plates and pipe a decorative frill over the joins. Scatter coarsely chopped pistachio nuts or walnuts over the frills, and dust with paprika. Garnish each plate with celery leaves and sprigs of mint or watercress.

Breads, Tarts and Quiches

Courgette and Pesto Pizza

SERVES 4

2 courgettes
1 packet pizza base mix
1 jar pesto sauce
2 tablespoons freshly grated
  Parmesan cheese

100g/4oz fresh mozzarella cheese
olive oil
salt and freshly ground pepper
basil leaves

1 Preheat the oven to 220°C/425°F/Gas 7. Slice the courgettes thinly, put them in a bowl and pour a little boiling water over them to soften. Meanwhile make a pizza base by adding 125ml/4 fl oz (blood heat) water to the dry mix and kneading it for 5 minutes until the dough has an elastic feel.

2 On a floured board, roll out the pizza base, either to make one large pizza or to go into four individual tart shells with removable bottoms. In either case stretch and form the dough with your fingers to create a raised rim round the edge of the pizza.

3 Flavour the pesto sauce with the Parmesan and spread a layer of this mixture over the bottom of the pizza base(s). Slice the mozzarella thinly. Arrange a layer of slices over the pesto sauce. Drain the courgette slices and place an overlapping layer over the mozzarella. Sprinkle with olive oil and season with freshly ground pepper.

4 Bake the pizza(s) in the centre of the oven (10 minutes for individual pizzas, 15–20 minutes for a large one). Garnish with fresh basil leaves.

Courgette Quiche

SERVES 4 AS A MAIN COURSE, 6 AS A STARTER

½ Spanish onion, finely chopped
3 tablespoons olive oil
2 small courgettes, thinly sliced
salt and freshly ground pepper
2 medium eggs
150ml/5 fl oz double cream

150ml/5 fl oz milk
freshly grated nutmeg
60g/1½oz finely grated Gruyère cheese
22cm/8½ inch pastry case, baked blind
(see below)

1 Preheat the oven to 170°C/325°F/Gas 3.

2 Sauté the finely chopped onion in the olive oil until soft, stirring constantly, so that it does not take colour. Remove from the pan with a slotted spoon and reserve.

3 Sauté the thinly sliced courgettes until lightly coloured. Season with salt and freshly ground pepper to taste. Remove from the pan with a slotted spoon and reserve.

4 Combine the eggs, double cream and milk and mix thoroughly. Season with salt, freshly ground pepper and freshly grated nutmeg to taste.

5 Sprinkle 2 tablespoons finely grated Gruyère into the bottom of the pastry case. Combine the onion and courgettes and spoon into the pastry case. Sprinkle with 2 tablespoons cheese. Pour in the egg and cream mixture and sprinkle with the remaining cheese. Bake the tart in the preheated oven for 30–40 minutes or until the custard is set and golden brown.

Baking blind: use a shortcrust pastry based on 150g/6oz flour or 185g/7oz made weight of frozen pastry. Baking blind keeps a chilled, unfilled pastry case from 'melting' down the side of your tin or bubbling up during baking. Line the pastry case with greaseproof paper or foil and weight it down with raw dried beans or rice (these can be re-used). Push the beans up against the sides of the pastry case to ensure that it is properly supported. Place the tin on a baking sheet and bake in an oven preheated to 200°C/400°F/Gas 6 for 10 minutes. Remove from oven and carefully lift out the greaseproof paper and beans or rice.

   Return the shell to the oven, turn the heat down to 180°C/350°F/Gas 4, and bake for just 8–10 minutes longer to dry out the base without allowing it to brown. If the pastry starts to brown around the edges, cover it lightly with foil.

Pepper Pissaladière

SERVES 4-6

22–23 cm/8½–9 inch pastry case,
  baked blind (see p. 207)
1 medium egg white, beaten
4 tablespoons freshly grated
  Parmesan cheese
5–6 tablespoons olive oil
450g/1lb ripe tomatoes, skinned and
  chopped, or 400g/14oz can peeled
  tomatoes, chopped

2 tablespoons tomato purée
½ teaspoon dried oregano
½ teaspoon sugar
salt and freshly ground pepper
3 Spanish onions, chopped
½ teaspoon dried thyme
50g/ 2oz butter
3 large sweet peppers (1 yellow, 1 green, 1 red)

1 Brush the half-baked pastry shell with beaten egg white and sprinkle with 2 table-spoons freshly grated Parmesan. Leave the pastry case in its tin on a baking sheet.

2 Heat 4 tablespoons olive oil in a heavy pan. Add the chopped tomatoes and tomato purée. Sprinkle with the dried oregano and sugar and season with salt and freshly ground pepper, to taste. Cook over a low heat for about 15 minutes or until excess moisture has evaporated. Stir and mash the tomato mixture with a wooden spoon to reduce to a thick purée. Stir in the remaining Parmesan. Allow to cool.

3 Sauté the chopped onions and dried thyme in the butter until transparent and very soft. Season with salt and freshly ground pepper and cool.

4 Preheat the oven to 180°C/350°F/Gas 4 and heat the grill, on its maximum setting.

5 When the grill is hot, lay the peppers in the grill pan and grill them as close to the heat as possible, turning frequently, until their skins are charred and blistered all over. Rub the skins off under cold running water. Cut the peppers in half, remove the cores, wash out the seeds and pat dry with absorbent paper. Cut each half into 3-4 strips.

6 Cover the prepared pastry case with the sautéed onions and spread the tomato mixture evenly over the top. Arrange the pepper strips on top, using their colours to best advantage.

7 Brush the top of the flan and the pepper strips with olive oil and bake in the preheated oven for 30 minutes. Serve hot or warm.

Roquefort Cream Quiche

SERVES 6

*25cm/10 inch pastry case,
baked blind (see p. 207)
150g/6oz Philadelphia cream cheese
75g/3 oz Roquefort cheese
25g/1oz butter, softened
3 medium eggs, well beaten*

*300ml/10 fl oz single cream
1 tablespoon chopped parsley
2 teaspoons chopped chives
salt and freshly ground pepper
sprig of parsley*

1 Leave the pastry case in its tin and place on a baking sheet. Preheat the oven to 190°C/375°F/Gas 5.

2 Turn the cream cheese into a mixing bowl, add the Roquefort and the softened butter and beat with a wooden spoon or mash with a fork until smoothly blended. Add the well-beaten eggs and single cream and blend thoroughly. Stir in the chopped herbs, and season very lightly with salt, if needed, and generously with freshly ground pepper.

3 Turn the cheese filling into the pastry case, smoothing it evenly. Bake the quiche for 25–30 minutes, until the filling is puffed up and light golden brown. Serve hot, lukewarm or cold, garnished with a sprig of parsley.

Melted Mozzarella and Parmesan Bites

SERVES 4

8 slices of brown bread, crusts removed	pinch of crushed dried chillies
4 tablespoons softened butter	2 tablespoons olive oil
100g/4oz Mozzarella cheese	Worcestershire sauce
4 tablespoons freshly grated	3 eggs, beaten
Parmesan cheese	vegetable oil, for frying
freshly ground pepper	red tomato salsa (see p. 219)

1 Preheat the oven to 110°C/220°F/Gas ¼. Spread 4 slices of bread with the softened butter. Cut the mozzarella into thin slices and arrange them in a single layer on the bread, leaving a 0.5cm/¼ inch margin all around the edge of the bread.

2 In a small bowl, combine the freshly grated Parmesan with freshly ground pepper, crushed dried chillies, olive oil and a few drops of Worcestershire sauce. Mix well and spread on the remaining 4 slices of bread, leaving 0.5cm/ ¼ inch margin all round. Place the prepared bread slices on top of the mozzarella, (spread side down) and press the edges firmly together.

3 Put the beaten eggs in a shallow soup plate and dip each sandwich in the egg to coat thoroughly all over. Make sure that the edges are well covered with the egg mixture so that they are well sealed.

4 Pour enough oil into a large heatproof frying pan to come to a depth of 4cm/1¼ inches. Heat gently until a cube of bread crust sizzles and turns golden brown when dropped into the oil. Fry the sandwiches two at a time, for 3–4 minutes on each side, until they are crisp and golden brown.

5 Drain thoroughly on absorbent paper and keep warm in the preheated oven while frying the remaining sandwiches. Serve immediately with red tomato salsa.

French Onion Tart

SERVES 4-6

23cm/9 inch pastry case, baked blind
   in a loose-bottomed tin
4 tablespoons butter
1 tablespoon olive oil
900g/2lb Spanish onions, very
   finely chopped

Cream Sauce
300ml/½ pint milk
1 bay leaf

1 clove
4 black peppercorns
½ vegetable stock cube, crumbled
1 tablespoon butter
1 ½ tablespoons flour
3 egg yolks
4 tablespoons freshly grated
   Parmesan cheese
salt and freshly ground pepper
freshly grated nutmeg

1 In a large, heavy-bottomed frying pan, melt the butter with the oil. Add the finely chopped onions and sauté gently, stirring constantly, until the onions have softened. Cover the pan, reduce the heat even further, and 'sweat' the onions for 10–15 minutes longer, stirring occasionally. They should be meltingly soft but not coloured.

2 Preheat oven to 180°C/350°F/Gas 4.

3 In a medium saucepan, combine the milk, bay leaf, clove, peppercorns and crumbled stock cube and bring gently to the boil over a moderate heat. Remove pan from heat; cover and leave the milk to infuse the flavours for 10–15 minutes. Strain into a jug.

3 In a larger saucepan, melt the butter. Add the flour and stir over a moderate heat for 2–3 minutes to make a smooth, pale roux. Whisk in the flavoured milk slowly and carefully to avoid making the sauce lumpy, and when it is smooth again, simmer for a further 3–4 minutes or until the sauce thickens and loses its raw, floury taste. Remove pan from the heat. Beat in the egg yolks, one at a time, followed by half the cheese. Season generously with salt, freshly ground pepper and a pinch of the nutmeg.

7 Drain off any liquid which may have collected in the pan with the onions and fold the onions gently into the sauce. Pour the onion mixture into the pre-baked pastry case and sprinkle with the remaining Parmesan.

8 Bake the tart for 25–30 minutes, or until the filling is set and golden brown on top. Serve hot or warm.

Glazed Onion Family Tart

SERVES 4-6

1 cooked French onion tart (see p. 211)
½ yellow pepper, cut into thin slices
½ red pepper, cut into thin slices

1 medium red onion, cut into 6 wedges
6 small spring onions, trimmed
6 large spring onions, trimmed

Glazed Vegetable Garnish
Your choice of 4 more of the following:
6 fat garlic cloves, peeled
6 little white onions, peeled and halved
12 silver onions, peeled
12 shallots, peeled
2 young leeks, cut into 6 segments each

Seasoned Butter for Glaze
8 tablespoons butter
1 vegetable stock cube, crumbled
1 teaspoon sugar
1 pinch each of saffron, ginger, cinnamon,
   paprika and cayenne pepper

1 Prepare the French onion tart as in the recipe on page 211. Remove the tart from the oven and turn the oven down to 170°C/325°F/Gas 3.

2 Poach the garlic cloves, halved white onions, silver onions and shallots in boiling salted water until just tender. Remove with a slotted spoon and reserve.

3 Poach the leek segments and red onion wedges in the same water until just tender. Remove with a slotted spoon and reserve. Add the spring onions to the saucepan (with the green tops out of the water) and poach until just tender. Remove and reserve.

4 To make the glaze, melt the butter with the crumbled stock cube, sugar and spices in a large frying pan.

5 Add the poached vegetables (one variety at a time) to the spiced butter and toss over a medium heat until coated. Remove each variety of glazed vegetables from the pan with a slotted spoon and arrange decoratively on the prepared French onion tart. Sauté the pepper strips in the spiced butter until tender. Remove with a slotted spoon and arrange on the tart to give colour contrast. Place the finished tart in the preheated oven to heat through for 10–15 minutes. Serve immediately.

Onion and Olive Pissaladière

SERVES 6

1.5kg/3lb yellow onions
4 tablespoons olive oil
225g/8oz bread dough
(or shortcrust pastry)

Garnish
50g/2oz tiny black olives
2 garlic cloves, finely chopped
1–2 teaspoons dried Herbes de Provence
olive oil

1 In a large heatproof frying pan (or large casserole), sauté the thinly sliced onions and finely chopped garlic in olive oil until transparent and just beginning to turn golden.

2 Preheat the oven to 180°C/350°F/Gas 4.

3 Roll out the bread dough (or pastry) on a floured work surface to a diameter of 25cm/10 inches. Place the dough on a lightly oiled baking tray. Spread the onion mixture on the dough, leaving a 0.5cm/¼ inch margin all round the edge of the dough. Garnish with a pinwheel of lines of little black olives radiating out from the centre of the tart. Sprinkle with dried Herbes de Provence and drizzle over a little olive oil.

4 Bake in the preheated oven for 40–45 minutes.

Carrot and Cheese Crostini

SERVES 4

150g/6oz soft mild cheese
  (such as Boursin)
150g/6oz cooked carrots (or same
  amount of cooked sweet potato)
sugar
olive oil
salt and freshly ground pepper
pinch of crushed dried chillies
4 slices olive ciabatta bread, cut
  1 cm/½ inch thick

1 cut garlic clove
1–2 canned pimentos, cut into
  thin strips
chopped fresh thyme (or oregano)

Garnish
8 small Little Gem salad leaves
12–16 black olives, soaked in olive oil
4–8 tomato wedges

1 Preheat the grill.

2 In the bowl of a food processor, combine equal quantities of soft cheese and canned carrots (or the same amount of cooked sweet potato). Add 2 tablespoons each sugar and olive oil and process until smooth, adding a little more olive oil, if necessary. Season the mixture with the salt and dried crushed chillies to taste, and process again.

3 Brush the slices of olive ciabatta bread on both sides with olive oil, and toast under grill until golden brown. Remove toasted bread slices from the grill and rub each slice with a cut clove of garlic.

4 Pipe the toasted bread slices with the carrot and cheese mixture and drizzle with olive oil. Top with a julienne of thinly sliced pimento tossed with chopped fresh thyme (or oregano) and olive oil, and pop under grill for a minute or two, or until lightly browned.

5 To serve, arrange the *crostini* on salad plates and garnish each serving with 2 small lettuce leaves, 3–4 black olives and a wedge or two of ripe tomato.

Wild Mushroom and Cheese Crescents

MAKES 20–24

butter
100g/4oz wild mushrooms (or Shiitake
  mushrooms), finely chopped
2 spring onions (green tops only),
  chopped
½ a packet Boursin herb and
  garlic cheese

freshly ground pepper
pinch of crushed dried chillies
350g/12oz shortcrust pastry
1 egg yolk, lightly beaten, to glaze
6 walnuts halves, chopped

1 Preheat the oven to 180°C/350°F/Gas 4. Lightly grease a baking sheet with 1 tablespoon softened butter.

2 Melt 2 tablespoons butter in a frying pan and gently fry the mushrooms for 3–4 minutes, or until the mushrooms are cooked through. Stir in the chopped spring onion tops and Boursin cheese; season generously with freshly ground pepper and crushed dried chillies and mix well. Chill.

3 Roll out the pastry on a lightly floured work surface to 0.5cm/¼ inch thickness. Using a round 7cm/3 inch pastry cutter (or the rim of a glass), cut out 20–24 pastry circles.

4 Place 1 teaspoonful of the mushroom and cheese mixture on one half of each circle. With your finger (or a small brush), moisten the edges of the pastry with a little cold water. Fold one side of each pastry circle over the filled side to form a semi-circle, pressing the pastry together firmly along the edges with your fingers. Then carefully form each semi-circle into a little crescent by gently pushing the ends together. Brush each crescent with a little beaten egg yolk, to glaze. Sprinkle with the chopped walnuts.

5 Place the crescents on the prepared baking sheet and bake in the preheated oven for about 40 minutes, or until the pastry is cooked and golden in colour. Serve immediately.

Cheese, Onion and Pepper Ring

SERVES 6

softened butter, to grease baking
  sheet
350g/12oz shortcrust pastry
150g/6oz packet Boursin herb and
  garlic cheese, chopped
2 onions, finely chopped
1 small red pepper, cored, seeded
  and finely chopped

2 spring onions (green parts only),
  finely chopped
salt and freshly ground pepper
pinch of crushed dried chillies
1 egg, beaten, to glaze

Garnish
tomato wedges, sprigs of watercress

1 Preheat the oven to 200°C/400°F/Gas 6. Grease a baking sheet with 1 tablespoon softened butter. Roll out the pastry on a lightly floured working surface to measure about 27x37cm/11x16 inches and 0.5cm/¼ inch thick. With a sharp knife, trim the edges of the pastry to form a neat rectangle.

2 In a bowl, combine the chopped cheese, onions, red pepper and spring onion tops. Season with salt, pepper and crushed dried chillies to taste and mix well. Chill.

3 Spread the cheese, pepper and onion mixture over the pastry, leaving 0.5cm/¼ inch margin all around the edges of the pastry. Brush 1 long edge of the pastry with beaten egg, and starting from the other long edge, roll up the pastry (like a Swiss roll) pressing along its length to seal the pastry edges firmly together.

4 Carefully transfer the roll (seam side down) to the baking sheet. Then, with a pair of kitchen scissors, cut along 1 edge at intervals of 2 inches, being careful not to cut more than a third of the way through the pastry roll. Shape the roll with a little beaten egg to hold the edges of the ring together.

5 Brush the surface of the pastry with beaten egg and bake the ring in the preheated oven for 35–40 minutes, or until the pastry is cooked and golden brown. Remove the baking sheet (and the pastry ring) from the oven and place on a cake rack to cool. When the pastry is cool enough to handle easily, transfer it to a serving dish and serve immediately, garnished with tomato wedges and sprigs of watercress.

Sauces and Salsas

Green Mayonnaise

300ml/½ pint thick, homemade
  mayonnaise
25g/1oz fresh parsley sprigs
25g/1 oz fresh watercress leaves
salt and freshly ground pepper

2 tablespoons finely chopped parsley
1 tablespoon finely chopped watercress
1 tablespoon finely chopped fresh tarragon
lemon juice

1 Prepare the mayonnaise with a flavouring of French mustard and lemon juice or wine vinegar.

2 Wash the parsley sprigs and watercress thoroughly.

3 Bring a pint of salted water to the boil. Plunge in the parsley and watercress, and boil for 6 minutes. Drain thoroughly, and press as dry as possible between the folds of a cloth.

4 Pound the blanched greens to a paste in a mortar. Run through a fine sieve to make a smooth purée.

5 Beat the purée into the mayonnaise, together with the finely chopped herbs, and if necessary correct the seasoning with more salt, freshly ground pepper and lemon juice.

6 Chill for a few hours before serving to allow the flavour of the herbs to develop.

Green Tartar Sauce

4 hard-boiled egg yolks
salt and freshly ground pepper
1 tablespoon vinegar
300ml/ ½ pint oil
4 tablespoons chives

1 Pass the egg yolks through a sieve. Mix them with salt, freshly ground pepper and vinegar and combine with the oil as for making a mayonnaise.

2 Liquidize the chives until very fine with a small spoonful of the mayonnaise mixture, pass through a fine sieve, then blend with the sauce.

Remoulade Sauce

300ml/ ½ pint mayonnaise
2 tablespoons each very finely chopped capers, gherkins and fine herbes
½ tablespoon mustard

1 Season the mayonnaise with the mustard.

2 Stir in the capers, gherkins and herbs.

Chantilly Sauce

300ml/ ½ pint mayonnaise
juice from ½ a lemon
3 tablespoons whipped cream

1 Combine the mayonnaise with lemon juice to taste.

2 Just before serving, fold in the whipped cream. Served with cold and lukewarm asparagus.

Horseradish Mayonnaise

300ml/ ½ pint mayonnaise
2–3oz horseradish

Combine the mayonnaise and horseradish.

Red Tomato Salsa

2 large beefsteak tomatoes, diced
1 large red pepper, seeded and diced
1 small red onion, peeled and
   finely diced
½ hot red chilli, seeded and sliced

2 tablespoons chopped coriander
4 tablespoons olive oil
1–2 tablespoons lime juice
salt

1 In a large bowl, combine the diced tomatoes, red pepper and red onion.

2 Add the thinly sliced hot red chilli , chopped coriander, olive oil, lime juice and salt to taste. Mix well and serve immediately.

Yellow Mango Salsa

1 large ripe mango, peeled, stoned
   and diced
1 large yellow pepper, seeded
   and diced
2 tablespoons lime juice

salt
1 small red onion, peeled and finely diced
½ hot red chilli, seeded and thinly sliced
4 tablespoons olive oil
2 tablespoons chopped coriander

1 In a bowl, combine the mango and yellow pepper with the lime juice and salt to taste.

2 Add the finely diced red onion and thinly sliced hot red chilli and mix well.

3 Stir in the olive oil and chopped coriander leaves and serve immediately.

Green Avocado, Kiwi and Cardamom Salsa

1 medium-sized avocado, ripe but firm
juice of 1 lime
2 kiwi fruits, peeled and diced
4 green cardamom seeds, crushed

4 tablespoons olive oil
salt
sugar
crushed dried chillies

1 With a sharp knife, carefully peel the ripe avocado. Cut the flesh into 0.5cm/¼ inch slices and then cut the slices into dice.

2 In a small bowl, combine the diced avocado with the lime juice, diced kiwi fruits, crushed cardamom seeds and olive oil. Add salt, sugar and crushed dried chillies to taste. Mix gently (to avoid mashing diced avocado) and serve immediately.

Corn and Pineapple Salsa

1 cob of corn
2–3 thin slices fresh pineapple
1 small red onion, peeled and
  finely diced

2 tablespoons lime juice
salt
sugar
crushed dried chillies

1   With a sharp knife, cut the kernels from the corn. In a small saucepan, steam the corn kernels in 4 tablespoons water until just tender. Remove from heat and drain.

2   Peel and core the pineapple slices and cut into small dice.

3   In a bowl, combine the prepared corn kernels and diced pineapple with the finely diced red onion, olive oil and lime juice. Season with salt, sugar and crushed dried chillies to taste. Mix well and serve immediately.

Madras Curry Sauce

2 tablespoons butter
1 medium onion, finely chopped
½ crumbled vegetable stock cube
1-2 tablespoons Madras curry powder
2 tablespoons flour
1-2 tablespoons tomato purée

salt and freshly ground pepper
300ml/½ pint milk
150ml/¼ pint double cream
lemon juice
salt, pepper
pinch of crushed dried chillies

1   Heat the butter in a saucepan, add the chopped onion and garlic and crumbled vegetable stock cube, and sauté until the vegetables are transparent. Stir in the curry powder and flour and cook for 3-4 minutes, stirring constantly. Then add the tomato purée and salt and freshly ground pepper, to taste. Mix well.

2   Stir in the milk and double cream and bring gently to the boil, stirring constantly to avoid lumps. Simmer the sauce over a gentle heat until it becomes thick enough just to coat the vegetables you wish to serve it with. Correct the seasoning, adding a little lemon juice, salt, pepper and crushed dried chillies (if desired) to taste.

Index

222